A PENGUIN SPECIAL

S198

WHAT'S WRONG WITH THE UNIONS?

ERIC WIGHAM

ERIC WIGHAM

What's Wrong With The Unions?

PENGUIN BOOKS

Penguin Books Ltd, Harmondsworth, Middlesex
U.S.A.: Penguin Books Inc., 3300 Clipper Mill Road, Baltimore 11, Md
AUSTRALIA: Penguin Books Pty Ltd, 762 Whitehorse Road,
Mitcham, Victoria

—

First published 1961

—

—

Made and printed in Great Britain
by Cox and Wyman Ltd,
London, Reading, and Fakenham

CONTENTS

PREFACE

MUCH of my daily work consists of writing about the activities of trade unions. I do it with temerity since I am a mere rank-and-file union member and have been, occasionally holding very minor office, for nearly thirty-five years. Moreover my union is one of those white-collar organizations which many union leaders regard with tolerant contempt.

But I make no apology for writing about unions or for criticizing them. 'The significance for the community generally of trade union policy and action is now such that no trade unionist should resent informed discussion and examination from outside the movement,' Mr Alan Birch, the chairman of the T.U.C. economic committee, has said. I believe that to be true and that there is nothing to prevent an observer from making himself informed. Trade unionists are ordinary people. Their ways and traditions are complicated, but not abnormally so.

No originality is claimed for the suggestions made at the end of this volume. Many of them have been put forward at one time or another in the newspaper by which I am employed. Some have been advocated or condemned by other writers.

The structure of the book is simple. Chapters 1 to 9 mention criticisms that have been made of trade unions, attempt to explain how the situation has come about, and describe what action, if any, has been taken to remedy defects. Chapter 10 is a sort of bonus for readers, since it is not about trade unions but shows that employers and their organizations are also imperfect. Chapter 11 lists all the criticisms and then discusses, one at a time, whether there is anything that ought to be done about them.

*

While I have not attempted to draw up a trade union bibliography, the reader may be interested in the following recent studies of some or all of the particular problems with which this book is concerned. Some are probably out of print.

PREFACE

The Daily Mirror Spotlight on Trade Unions, by Sydney Jacobson and William Connor. Daily Mirror, 3*d*. (1956).

Structure of the British Trade Union Movement, by Alan Birch. Manchester Statistical Society, 5*s*. (1957).

Trade Unions and the Individual, by Cyril Grunfeld. Fabian Society, 3*s*. (1957).

A Giant's Strength, by the Inns of Court Conservative and Unionist Society (1958).

The Trade Unions, three articles in the *Economist* in February 1958, and *The Anatomy of British Trade Unions*, two articles in the same journal in February 1959.

Trade Unions in a Free Society, by B. C. Roberts. Institute of Economic Affairs, 9*s*. 6*d*. (1959).

The Bargainers, by George Cyriax and Robert Oakeshott. Faber & Faber, 21*s*. (1960).

Finally, I must express my gratitude to Mr Hugh Chevins and Mr John Walton for reading and criticizing my manuscript. They are in no way to blame for its contents.

ERIC WIGHAM

INTRODUCTION

*Heads or Tails – The Turning Point – Woodcock's Warning –
Above the Law – Their Own Image*

WHAT is right with British trade unions far outweighs what is wrong.

At their best they stand for much that is valuable in the British character, indeed much that is valuable in the human race. The qualities they demand and develop are comradeship and loyalty, willingness to serve without regard, respect for tradition, resoluteness, the dignity of working men, acceptance of majority decisions and the tolerance that goes with it, the understanding and exercise of all that we mean when we talk about the democratic way of life.

But there are times when the reverse side of the penny shows itself, when comradeship becomes conspiracy for selfish gain, when loyalty becomes sheeplikeness, when unpaid service turns to officiousness and even bullying, when respect for tradition turns to rigidity, resoluteness to obstinacy, dignity to insolence, acceptance of majority decisions to subservience, tolerance to irresponsibility, and democracy comes near to anarchy. How one looks at it, of course, depends partly on the eye of the beholder and partly on the circumstances in which the qualities are exercised. Motives are always mixed; judgement is never unerring.

One must feel some admiration for a man who sacrifices his wages to strike in support of a fellow-worker, when he has nothing to gain by it. But admiration is tempered by impatience when the fellow-worker is irresponsibly breaking an agreement or when a striker leaves his work, as sometimes happens, without even knowing what the dispute is about.

'My fellow-worker, right or wrong' is a doctrine almost as emotive as 'my country, right or wrong', but as little to be justified on any moral principle. Loyalty or 'solidarity' is the basis on which trade unions are built, but the loyalty may be narrow or wide, far-sighted or short-sighted. Loyalties may conflict, loyalty to immediate fellow-workers with loyalty to a union, loyalty to a union with loyalty to the trade union movement as a whole, loyalty to the movement with loyalty to the country, loyalty to the country with loyalty to the workers of the world. A choice has frequently to be made. In two world wars, the trade unions have demonstrated that they find national loyalties overriding. In hundreds of unofficial strikes and numerous demarcation disputes every year, groups of workers demonstrate their attachment to the narrowest ties.

The trade unions, by their long history of struggle, have attracted the sympathy felt by most people of goodwill in modern times for the champion of the underdog, but they have always had their faults and their weaknesses. In the early days of the industrial revolution, when infants crawled in the mills for sixteen hours a day and half-naked women sweated in the mines, it was illegal for workers to combine for self-protection. There was heroism then in the men who met secretly by night, never in the same place twice, dedicating themselves by fearsome oaths, daily risking imprisonment and the employers' black list which would make it impossible to earn a living. But there were also hungry men then, driven to desperation, who resorted to machine-wrecking, vitriol-throwing, even murder.

There was a noble and pathetic idealism in the wave of trade unionism in the eighteen-thirties, when foolish men rushed to disaster dreaming they could transform society in a day. There was dignity and toughness in the men who built the new model unions of the eighteen-fifties and sixties, solidly organized and financed craft organizations which could face employers' attacks again and again without breaking. But, while Marx was calling on the workers of the world to unite, they were securing their position partly at the expense of the unskilled workers whose membership they refused and whose poverty they ignored.

Few could withhold their sympathy when at last, from 1889 onwards, the bottom dogs were roused to action, the unskilled labouring masses who for generations had lived on the verge of destitution. But they turned their minds to syndicalist revolution and fought great industrial battles before and after the First World War, until they came to the crowning folly of the General

Strike in 1926. That taught the unions to be patient, even while young men rotted at street corners and hunger marchers tramped the roads.

After the Second World War, the unions tried valiantly to face the new problems of full employment. Instead of fighting for all the money they could get, they tried for two and a half years to restrain their members from excessive claims. They voluntarily accepted compulsory arbitration and the continued outlawing of strikes. They collaborated with employers to increase productivity. They discouraged restrictive practices. Some unions could not face up to it. Some groups of workers rebelled in unofficial strikes. It was not surprising that they did. The marvel was that the movement as a whole was able so quickly to reverse two centuries of tradition. They probably could not have done it if there had not been a friendly Government in office, pursuing the economic policies they advocated, making full employment a priority, trying to keep prices down by subsidies and other means, trying to control the economy, nationalizing basic industries, taxing profits, introducing major social reforms.

There was plenty of criticism of the unions but on the whole they retained the sympathy of a public which understood something of their difficulties. Nor did the T.U.C. at once display hostility to the Conservative Government, when it was returned. Indeed, immediately after the 1951 General Election the T.U.C. General Council, the central executive body of the trade union movement, declared: 'It is our long-standing practice to seek to work amicably with whatever Government is in power and through consultation jointly with Ministers and with the other side of industry to find practical solutions to the social and economic problems facing this country.' They warned their members against any attempt to resist Government measures by industrial action.

The unions had become in a very real sense a part of 'the establishment'. Their association with the Government and employers on scores of committees of all kinds and their accepted right to be consulted on any subject affecting their members directly or indirectly made them an important influence in the nation's councils and also, many people felt, imposed a responsibility on them. They had become a part of the body of the State in many of its intricate ramifications, instead of being, as they once were, something outside the State and in some senses a rival power. It was therefore their duty, people instinctively felt, and most of their leaders felt, to help to keep the body healthy. Belonging, as they now did, implied loyalty. The movement has never fully realized all that is involved in that, and indeed sections have been constantly struggling to break free. But it was partly because they had been so closely woven into the fabric of the community, that the rents they made in the fabric were later so much resented.

For several years of Conservative Government reasonably amicable relations were maintained, however. The unions were naturally critical of a number of Government measures, such as the denationalization of steel and road haulage and the removal of controls and subsidies, but real wages were rising, the Government maintained the intricate consultative machine, and Sir Walter (now Lord) Monckton was the most tactful of Ministers of Labour. The T.U.C. opposed the Government policy in a responsible way.

The turning point came in the next election year, 1955. There was a succession of major strikes that year – on the docks, the railways, national newspapers – which were in great measure due to quarrels between unions. Arthur Deakin and his successor died, to be succeeded by Mr Frank Cousins. The unions were angry about what they regarded as political dishonesty on the part of the Government in producing an 'easy' pre-election Budget and a stiff one in October. From that point relations with the Government deteriorated. They were exacerbated by the measures taken to prevent inflation, which the unions considered short-sighted and unjust and which, during the London bus strike of 1958, came nearer to producing an all-out clash than anything since the General Strike of 1926.

No one would blame the trade unions for being critical of the way a Government behaves, but the result of their hostility was to produce an atmosphere of irresponsibility, almost of reckless-ness. While Frank Cousins denounced wage restraint to the plaudits of the Trades Union Congress, other leaders were reduced to sullen silence. In times of war, looting and atrocities can be restrained only by strict discipline. Discipline in the trade union movement was far from strict.

The public was shocked by exposures of the way some members of the trade union movement were behaving at workshop and branch level. Public inquiries revealed little tyrannous empires of shop stewards or branch officials at London Airport, Briggs Motor Bodies, London markets, and elsewhere. There were some violent incidents involving damage to vehicles during strikes, for instance that of the provincial busmen in 1957. There were examples of individuals being persecuted by their unions or fellow-workers. A series of absurd demarcation disputes interrupted work at some of the shipyards.

Unofficial strikes, which were understandable if reprehensible in the period of wage restraint and compulsory arbitration, continued to occur constantly in some sections of industry though for most of them little excuse remained. There were accusations of unscrupulous behaviour by Communists in the unions. And all the time wage claims were large and unceasing and offers of arbitration by employers were frequently refused.

All this can be exaggerated. There were faults on the part of Government and employers as well as of the workers. It is still true that over the greater part of British industry labour relations are reasonably good. The union leaders are experienced and for the most part responsible men. Only a few employers' organizations regard restrictive practices as a serious problem. Persecution is rare. The amount of working time lost in strikes still compares favourably with most of the other major industrial countries, particularly the United States. There are no political strikes such as are common in some Continental countries. The Communists are on the whole losing ground. Corruption is almost unknown. There is active collaboration at the top to increase productivity.

It would be a mistake to think of unions in terms only of national leaders and national negotiations, still more a mistake to think of them in terms only of such things as closed shop, victimization, and demarcation disputes. The basic strength

13

and character of the movement are given to it by its half a million voluntary workers.

There may be a few hundred troublesome shop stewards, but there are probably 200,000 altogether, carrying out day after day a hard job without reward. If they collect subscriptions, they may be allowed to keep a small percentage, but that is all. They collect money, distribute ballot papers for elections, help to distribute the union journal, see new recruits and get them into the union if they can, but most important is their task of settling the constant little problems that arise with the management – talking over piecework rates with a foreman if the worker is not satisfied, keeping an eye on safety precautions, sorting out duty rota complaints, and nearly always settling them on the shop floor.

Thousands more workers are members of joint consultative committees, discussing all kinds of questions with the management – the running of the canteen, leisure activities, transport to the factory, everything that affects the workers' lives except wages and hours of work, and if it is a good committee also discussing things like suggestion schemes, the firm's plans for the future, and how to get the work done more efficiently.

Tens of thousands more do unpaid work as branch secretaries or chairmen or treasurers, dull, administrative work which few people find attractive but which someone is always found to do. Very big branches may have a paid secretary, but in most he just gets an honorarium of a few pounds a year.

The unions live now as they have always done, by the patient work, day in and day out, without thanks or reward, of thousands of decent working people in the factories and mines, on building sites and ships and buses and trains, in fact wherever the nation's work is done. Little is heard of their work but industry would find it hard to do without them.

Nevertheless the evidence here and there of irresponsibility and abuse of power has had its effect on the public mind. According to a Gallup poll, whereas only twelve per cent of the people thought trade unions a bad thing in 1954, twenty-three per cent thought them a bad thing in 1959. What most disturbs the public is probably not so much the fact that abuses occasionally occur, as that responsible union leaders seem to do so little to stop them.

The unions have become increasingly aware of their growing unpopularity. At first they affected to attribute all criticism to malice or ignorance, but it became increasingly hard for them to persuade themselves that that was the whole explanation. In the summer of 1959, Mr George Woodcock, the present T.U.C. general secretary, a man not given to self-deception, gave a frank talk on the subject in the B.B.C. third programme.

He found one sign of declining sympathy with unions in the changed attitude of the courts. Formerly, recognizing that unions were voluntary societies of working men for mutual aid, they had tended to discourage legal action by members complaining of harsh treatment or breach of rule. But about 1950, according to Mr Woodcock, their attitude changed. There were several cases in which individual members obtained the protection of the courts and in some cases were awarded damages against the union itself.

One reason for this, Mr Woodcock suggested, might be that the courts had decided, in view of the spread of the closed shop, that the time had come when a workman's right to be in the union and his rights inside the union needed to be carefully safeguarded.

Mr Woodcock went on to suggest that the change in the attitude of the courts reflected the change in the attitude of the general public, the main reason in both cases being the increase in the power of the trade unions since the end of the war. Trade unions had lost the sympathy the public reserve for the underdog because they no longer gave the impression of being underdogs. Mr Woodcock mentioned four particular trade union practices which he thought many people found particularly disturbing – unofficial disputes, demarcation disputes, noisy demonstrations by trade unionists on strike, and the closed shop.

'In many cases,' Mr Woodcock concluded, 'the responsible head officers of the unions whose members are concerned dislike these things and could stop them if they were determined to do so. I believe they should make the effort, for it is neither fair to the bulk of ordinary trade unionists nor wise in the interests of the trade union movement to allow an undisciplined minority to get the unions a bad name.'

During the summer of 1959 there were other signs of trade union impatience with abuses of union power, and the General Council announced to the Congress that they proposed to conduct an inquiry into unofficial strikes and the behaviour of shop stewards. They duly reported in 1960, criticizing unofficial shop steward activities, and afterwards there were indications that some large unions were making greater efforts to maintain discipline and establish closer contact with their rank-and-file members.

No doubt the unions were driven to action partly by the fear that, if they did nothing, the Government would act.

All union leaders who discussed the subject started from the premise that any effort to remedy the situation by legislation was undesirable. 'The danger that the unions have to guard against', said Mr Woodcock, 'is that the public may turn against trade unions to such an extent as to demand that the unions should be restrained from outside – by laws which restrict or prohibit activities that are ridiculous or oppressive.'

More and more people outside the movement, however, were beginning to wonder whether it would not be a good thing, even from the point of view of the unions themselves, to introduce some legal remedy. No doubt if unions never indulged in such activities it would not be necessary, but perfection cannot be expected from unions any more than from any other type of organization. Occasional abuses are inevitable, unless steps are taken to prevent them.

At present unions are protected from retribution for most such abuses by their unique legal position. In some ways they are accurately said to be 'above the law'. Certainly there are not the safeguards either for the public or for the individual member which have been thought necessary for many other types of organization.

The basis of trade unionism as we know it today is the Trade Union Act of 1871, which laid down that unions would no longer be illegal because they were in restraint of trade and, under a system of voluntary registration, gave them the right to take proceedings to protect their funds. Four years later the Conspiracy and Protection of Property Act permitted joint action in contemplation or furtherance of a trade dispute unless such action by an individual would have been punishable as a crime.

In 1901, the Taff Vale judgement by the House of Lords held that a union could be sued in a Civil Court for damages for wrongs done by its agents during a strike. Union funds were in danger. The result was the Trade Disputes Act, 1906, which said that no action could be taken against any union in respect of any wrong committed by or on behalf of the union, whether or not in connexion with a trade dispute. The Act also said that an act done by a person in connexion with a trade dispute should not be actionable on the ground that it induced some other person to break a contract of employment.

Their actual legal position is much more complicated than that makes it sound, partly as a result of a series of subsequent legal judgements, but it is true to say that laws have been passed specially to make it legal for them to do things that would otherwise be illegal and to relieve them from having to pay damages for acts which would otherwise have laid them open to damages.

In return for this privileged position, unions are subjected to few legal restrictions. They were given their special status because they were weak. The aim was to create a fair balance of power in industry. But now they are much stronger. They have become an essential part of the economic fabric of the state, consulted and respected by Governments, recognized and often feared by employers. Their collective bargaining position has been greatly strengthened by full employment. In many plants and some industries they have established a closed shop, which gives them power over the livelihood of workers. Has not the time come, it is often asked, to introduce legislation to ensure that all this power is not abused?

At present there is no regulation of their non-political activities unless they are registered, but most of them are because registration gives them some legal advantages. The obligations imposed even on a registered union are very light, however. It must submit to the Chief Registrar of Friendly Societies copies of its rules, which must include among other things the objects of the union, the penalties which may be imposed on members, the method of appointment and removal of a general committee of management and officers, but neither the law nor the Registrar lays down how the rules shall deal with these various matters, and constitutions vary widely. Finally, they are obliged to make an annual return to the Registrar.

Having issued a certificate of registration, the Registrar has no authority to ensure that the rules are carried out, though in his annual report he sometimes draws attention to actions by unions which he regards as undesirable. In recent reports, for instance, he has criticized unions for employing unqualified auditors and for failing to prosecute when there is reason to suspect mis-appropriation of funds. Members of a union may have recourse to the courts to stop misapplication of rules and in some cir-cumstances to sue for damages.

There is regulation of the political activities of unions under the Trade Union Act, 1913, which gives members the right to appeal to the Registrar for a final decision if they believe that a rule has been misapplied. Should his powers of supervision over the non-political activities of unions be extended?

The Registrar already has considerable powers in relation to other voluntary organizations, such as cooperative societies and building societies. Disputes between members and their society may be referred to him or some other arbitrator and the decision can be enforced by the county court. The Registrar may also order an inspection and report on the affairs of a society, or call a special general meeting, on the application of one tenth of the members, or of 100 members if the society has more than 1,000.

The object of what follows is not to question the desirability of strong trade unions, able to bargain with employers on terms of equality and to play an influential part in the economic life of the nation. The object is to look at some of the reasons for the public impression that they are playing that part inadequately or that they are abusing their privileged position and, in so far as the impression appears to be justified, to consider what reme-dies may be applied.

A point to be borne in mind is that the unions have set exceptionally high standards for themselves and to a large extent are judged on those standards. Employers have made their profit-motive their god and are never tired of asserting that management will not do a good job unless there is an adequate financial incentive. I am certain that they under-estimate their own qualities, but the result of accepting such mercenary standards is that the public do not regard it as a matter of complaint when they appear to be interested only in money.

The unions, however, have always talked about things like the brotherhood of man and common service to the community. So when they fall short of these standards in action, as inevitably they constantly do, they are criticized for it. There seems to be a general feeling that it is creditable for an employer to make as much profit as he can but wicked and selfish for a worker to get as high wages as he can.

But though their standards are so different, they are in fact the same sort of people with the same qualities and failings. An impartial observer should try to apply common standards in judging their achievements and failures.

1

THE LOST LEADERS

Vacuum at the Centre – Departed Giants? – The Acquisitive
Boards – Too Much to Do – Unionism on the Cheap

If trade union leaders were supermen they would rapidly solve
the problems of the movement. But they would not need to be
supermen to remedy gradually but steadily the deficiencies that
have appeared, if they shared a common constructive purpose.
The movement is a democratic one and the leaders have no power
beyond what their members give them, but narrowness of vision
and out-of-date traditions can be worn away by persistent and
courageous exposition of enlightened policies. To some extent
that has been and is happening, but slowly. The leadership is not
keeping pace with the march of events.

That is no doubt partly because there has in recent years been
no central leadership with authority. The T.U.C. General Council
can provide that central leadership even though it cannot control
the policies of individual unions, of which the general secretaries
or full-time presidents are themselves subject to executive committees, which in their turn are responsible to rank-and-file
opinion expressed through national conferences, branch resolutions, and, sometimes, through unofficial strikes and other forms
of indirect pressure.

The leaders of the half dozen biggest unions, who hold half the
votes at Congress, are in a position to decide the policy of the
T.U.C., if backed by their own organizations, and to exercise
a great influence on the policy of the whole movement. From the
end of the Second World War until the death of Mr Arthur
Deakin on May Day, 1955, the policy of the T.U.C. was for
practical purposes controlled by a triumvirate consisting of Mr
Deakin, the general secretary of the Transport and General
Workers' Union, Sir William Lawther, president of the National
Union of Mineworkers, and Mr (now Sir Thomas) Williamson,

general secretary of the National Union of General and Municipal Workers. All three were assured of the backing of their executives. They had between them about one third of the votes at the Annual Congress, and could count on the support of a number of middle-sized unions for their right-wing policies on such matters as wage restraint, measures to increase productivity, and nationalization. Mr (now Sir Lincoln) Evans was their able spokesman on economic affairs. Sir Vincent Tewson, then general secretary of the T.U.C., was their willing lieutenant.

They could by their block votes pretty well decide who was elected to the General Council, and consequently some leaders of smaller unions took pains to avoid causing them offence. Mr Deakin, the dominating figure in the triumvirate, was surrounded by sycophants as well as like-thinking allies. The power of the triumvirate was much weakened in 1950, when the annual Trades Union Congress finally threw off the policy of wage restraint. This was not due to a break-up of the triumvirate, however, but to their attempt through the General Council to put through proposals for a wage standstill against which the membership rebelled. Both the miners and the distributive workers reversed the policy of their leaders.

After Mr Frank Cousins became general secretary of the Transport and General Workers' Union in 1956, the T.U.C. was leaderless. There could hardly have been a more convincing demonstration of the power of an able general secretary in some unions than the complete change in the policy of Transport and General after Mr Cousins' assumption of power. In the twinkling of an eye the bulwark of the right became the spearhead of the non-Communist left – and not only in the T.U.C. In federations and joint union bodies, T.G.W.U. representatives underwent an overnight conversion. The national executive council became as predominantly left as before it had been predominantly right, whether the issue were nuclear weapons, nationalization, or wages.

It may be conceded that the development of the Conservative Government's economic policy after 1955 might have revealed different aspects of Mr Deakin's character, if he had still been there, but it is impossible to believe his policy would have had any resemblance to that of Mr Cousins.

The change destroyed the basis of the old leadership, but put nothing in its place. Mr Cousins made no attempt to create a new ruling group on the left, alienating even would-be supporters by his unpredictability and failures in judgement, and sometimes appearing to regard the whole General Council, and especially Sir Vincent Tewson, with contempt.

On the other hand, the right wing failed to steady its ranks. Other changes had been taking place. In 1958 Mr Alan Birch, of the distributive workers, one of the few members of the General Council who has given serious thought to the possibility of coordinating trade union policy, became chairman of the economic committee. His ideas were regarded with no less suspicion by Mr Harry Douglass, of the steelworkers, on the right, than by Mr Cousins on the left.

Mr Jim Campbell, general secretary of the National Union of Railwaymen who also had ideas about revising the structure of the movement, was killed in a road accident in the Soviet Union in 1957 and was replaced by Mr Sydney Greene, more orthodox of mind and hampered by an executive which has out-voted him more than once on important issues. Sir William Lawther was succeeded by Mr Ernest Jones, more earnestly to the right than Sir William but less shrewd and less able to carry his union with him. Jones retired in 1960 and in the same year Mr Paynter, the Communist general secretary of the miners, became a member of the T.U.C. General Council. The only remaining member of the triumvirate is Sir Thomas Williamson, who is not a dominating figure of the Deakin type.

Meanwhile a new potential leader of the right appeared in Mr William Carron, president of the Amalgamated Engineering Union, who is in a much stronger position on his executive than were his predecessors in the union, but handicapped by a small delegate conference, known as the 'national committee', which is often unable to counter the manoeuvres of its Communist minority and makes many irresponsible decisions.

With the right thus changing, divided, and confused, it is no wonder that they failed to maintain the Deakin tradition. There have been times when they appeared to throw up the sponge. At Congress after Congress, from 1956 onwards, they sat glumly in their places while delegates acclaimed economic policies of which they disapproved. Rather than face the possibility of defeat, they kept silence, often leaving difficult issues to a 'free vote' of the Congress, with an exaggerated fear of bringing their divisions into the open.

The new pattern which will follow the succession of Mr George Woodcock to the general secretaryship of the T.U.C. in September 1960 has yet to show itself.

If the national union leaders have been failing to meet their very difficult responsibilities, is it because the calibre of union leaders has deteriorated? Past leaders are always magnified by the mists of time. But when one comes down to it, were they such giants in the old days? Were they giants who formed and then broke up the triple alliance of miners, railwaymen, and transport workers in 1921? Were they giants who stumbled into the General Strike in 1926 and then backed out of it? Was there not greater wisdom among the men who refused to extend the London bus strike in 1958?

It is sometimes said that a race of stalwart fighters has given place to a race of committee men and office-chair administrators. The same thing was being said in the 1870s. Indeed the foundations of the trade union movement were laid by the men who built the 'new model' craft unions about a century ago on the basis of sound administration, careful finance, and the avoidance of conflict where possible. It was the employers who forced the big battles of those days.

It is true that a new race of barnstormers grew up with the general unions from 1889 onwards, but by the time of the great amalgamations of the early 1920s, which created the giant unions we know today, their job was largely done. In any case they did not always impress their contemporaries.

'The leading men have grown fatter in body and even more dully complacent in mind than they were twenty years ago,' wrote Beatrice Webb in her diary of the 1915 T.U.C. congress. 'The delegates have lost their keenness. The rebels of today don't get elected to Congress and the "old hands" know, from long experience, that it is more of an "outing" than a gathering for

24

the transaction of working-class affairs. . . . The absence of intellectual leadership or consciousness of a common policy is really deplorable. The same old hackneyed sectional resolutions are languidly discussed and mechanically passed; and, in so far as there is any feeling, it is reserved for jealousy between leaders or for disputes between rival unions.'

Few of the T.U.C. leaders of today have spent their lives at office desks. The average age of the members of the General Council is a little over fifty-six. None were more than boys during the period of most bitter industrial strife before the First World War but most were active young unionists during the turbulent twenties, having left school at fourteen and entered their unions a year or two later. The battle for recognition had largely been won but other battles were still being fought. No doubt at lower levels in the hierarchy there are many who know only the relatively peaceful industrial era that has followed 1926, but that generation has yet to take over.

How a man has reached the top matters less than whether he has the stuff of leadership in him. Since the First World War the trade union movement has produced two great men – Ernest Bevin and Walter Citrine. One came up the hard way, overcoming every obstacle. The other was essentially a trade union Civil Servant.

The unions lost them both – Bevin to politics, Citrine to the board of a nationalized industry. This loss of union leaders to public employment has been an important cause of the weakness in union leadership since the war.

Even the loss of union leaders to public employment is nothing new, however. John Prior, general secretary of the Amalgamated Society of Carpenters, became a factory inspector in 1881, and a number of others went into Government service in the years that followed.

After the 1867 Reform Act, trade union leaders began to enter Parliament, first as Liberals, later as Labour Party members. Eventually, the loss of union leaders to politics became a serious matter, and many large unions now have rules forbidding their chief officers to sit in Parliament. Had it not been for the exceptional circumstances of the war, and the exceptional qualities of the man, Bevin would never have become a Minister. A small number of secretaries of smaller unions are Members of Parliament, but most trade union M.P.s come from the lower ranks. A political career is regarded as an alternative to a trade union career, not the culmination or concomitant of it. Apart from Mr Bevin, the T.U.C. General Council's only loss to Parliament in recent years was the appointment of Mr George Isaacs to be Minister of Labour in 1945.

Comparatively few trade union leaders at any time have entered private industry. To do so is regarded by many unionists as a kind of apostasy.

To go over to a nationalized industry is a different matter. The T.U.C. has always insisted that nationalization boards should include men with trade union experience, though not in a representative capacity, and consequently felt in duty bound, when the Labour Government was carrying through its nationalization programme, to encourage union leaders to accept such positions – though it cannot be said union negotiators always welcome the sight of former colleagues on the other side of the negotiating table, however much they may approve in principle.

The losses of the T.U.C. General Council to the boards of nationalized industries since the war have been serious. They include, besides Walter Citrine, at least ten full-time presidents or general secretaries of important unions, several of whom had also been chairmen of General Council committees. Many others at lower levels were lost to national, regional, or area boards.

The most serious of these losses were those of Citrine and James Bowman, who eventually became, respectively, chairman of the Central Electricity Authority and chairman of the National Coal Board. Citrine had been general secretary of the T.U.C. for twenty years. With a firm but sensitive hand, he had guided the organization patiently and persistently towards ever-increasing prestige and influence both inside and outside the movement. He knew just when to give way to gusts of opinion on the General Council but always returned to his original direction when they blew themselves out. He was well aware of the suspicion felt by union leaders of any apparent encroachment on their independence by the T.U.C. and he edged forward by almost imperceptible stages, a little here, a little there, always improving the standing and influence of the central body. The report on postwar policy published in 1944 is a monument to his far-sightedness and ability to think out the problems facing the movement. Had he stayed until he reached the age of retirement he would have had six more years as general secretary. His guiding hand, acting as a counter-weight to Deakin's domination, would have been invaluable in those vital first years of peace.

His successor, Sir Vincent Tewson, was as honest, sincere, and well-meaning a man as any in the movement, but slow to make up his mind, ultra-cautious, negative, lacking in the constructive ability and drive required to push the General Council along a set course.

Jim Bowman was obviously the most promising young man on the General Council when he left. He was one of the few – perhaps the only one from a big union – who had demonstrated the courage and ability to stand up to Deakin. He was the natural successor to Sir William Lawther as the miners' president and might well have become the outstanding union leader of his day.

A serious loss for quite different reasons was that of E. W. Bussey. As president of the Electrical Trades Union, he was almost the only remaining obstacle to complete Communist control of that union. His departure let Frank Foulkes into the presidency of the first big union to be wholly run by Communists. Perhaps it was already too late to save the E.T.U., but it is interesting to speculate on what might have happened had he stayed to fight a rearguard action to the end.

Some of the rest were approaching retirement when they departed and were succeeded by men of similar stamp, though on the whole probably of somewhat lesser calibre.

Most unions have fixed sixty-five (some sixty) as the retiring age for their officials and an appointment to the board of a nationalized industry is attractive to a union leader of sixty-two or sixty-three who feels he has a good many years of active life in front of him, particularly if his union is prepared to be accommodating, as it usually is, about his pension rights.

The financial aspect is important. The salaries of trade union officials are low in relation to their responsibilities and the size of the organizations they administer. Some of the white-collar unions pay relatively well. The general secretary of the National and Local Government Officers' Association, for instance, was appointed on a salary scale rising from £3250 to £4000, later increased. The Institution of Professional Civil Servants raised their general secretary's salary to £4000 in 1960. But the manual workers' unions – and some white-collar ones – are traditionally bad employers.

Mr George Woodcock was appointed T.U.C. general secretary in 1960 with a salary of £2850 a year. The biggest union of all, the Transport and General Workers, and the National Union of Railwaymen were both paying their general secretaries a little over £2200. The National Union of General and Municipal Workers were believed to pay rather more than that and the Union of Shop, Distributive and Allied Workers rather less. The miners paid their president and general secretary £1750 each.

Perhaps the meanest of all is the Amalgamated Engineering Union. In 1960 there was a proposal to raise the pay of their president and general secretary from £1280, including a personal allowance of £100, to £1600. Incredible as it may seem, the national committee at first refused to give them any increase at all. However they had second thoughts and allowed them £120, the same increase that was given to all other full-time officials.

In some cases additions worth two or three hundred pounds a year must be made for provision of cars, houses, or allowances of various kinds.

Members of the National Coal Board and British Transport Commission at that time were getting £7500 a year and their chairmen £10,000 each. The remuneration of big industrialists was of course much higher still. While allowances for expenses may help union leaders to meet some of their responsibilities, they are not comparable with the expenses paid in industry.

The leadership is weak not only, perhaps not mainly, because the men who come to the top are not of the necessary calibre. Too many of them are not; but, while there is no Bevin or Citrine on the T.U.C. General Council today, there are probably a dozen or more men of some stature. The trouble is that too much is expected of them. They have their own unions to run, which in itself might be thought a full-time job, with their executive and other meetings, conferences, negotiations, and strikes, the administrative problems, and the constant demand to address meetings up and down the country.

They have to attend the meetings of the General Council and its committees, and very likely meetings of the federations and similar bodies to which they belong. They probably represent the General Council on one or more of the Government advisory bodies and are sure to be on some of the 100 or so outside committees on which the T.U.C. is represented. They may be appointed to courts of inquiry or Royal Commissions. Some of them go abroad to international trade union meetings. Every summer the business of the General Council languishes while ten or so of its members spend five weeks at the International Labour Conference.

And in addition to all this some of the most influential leaders take part-time jobs on nationalization boards or other public bodies, which will supplement their incomes. They can well argue that in doing so they are serving the movement, but these jobs take up time that is already over-crowded.

The meetings which trade union officials have to attend are not only far too numerous but far too varied. No one who looks at the annual report of the T.U.C. General Council can fail to be astonished at the enormous spread of the subjects which they discuss and on which they make decisions.

Every year they adjudicate on anything up to a dozen disputes between unions. The range of the organization committee is wide enough to cover problems of the Carlisle state public house scheme, prison competition for municipal contracts, registration of theatrical employers, and a Government inquiry into the Truck Acts. The social insurance and industrial welfare committee ranges over every facet of the welfare state, from national superannuation to poliomyelitis vaccination and water fluoridation. The education committee is concerned not only with trade union education, as such, including the T.U.C.'s own college and other activities, but with every current national educational problem and the training of young workers. Hardly an international or colonial issue of the year escapes the attention of the international committee, though it is busy enough with its own international relations in the International Confederation of Free Trade Unions and the International Labour Organization. The production committee is concerned with productivity, work study courses, aspects of industrial policy, and the activities of numerous organizations concerned with management techniques and practices, while the scientific advisory committee involves itself in the work of research associations and developments in nuclear power and automation. The economic committee, usually regarded as the most important, keeps a constant critical watch on Government economic policy and on the economic pulse of the nation, while finding time for a myriad other things such as proposals for nationalization, speed regulations, public trusts for opera, car allowances for Government committees, agricultural marketing boards, and coastal protection.

And when all these are encompassed, the report has yet to include the work of the Press and Publications Section, and numerous miscellaneous items which may vary from the affairs of the Electrical Trades Union to the presentation of a painting by the Labour Party and the report of the delegate to the Co-operative Congress.

In the body of the report, almost every year, is the text of the detailed evidence submitted by the T.U.C. to various Government inquiries and commissions and usually there is at least one comprehensive inquiry conducted into some aspect of the affairs of the trade union movement itself. Often there are one or two long appendices.

This is the astonishing scope of the work of thirty-five men almost all of whom· have major responsibilities to their own unions and other outside commitments. Obviously they cannot be well informed on every item. Obviously they can seldom have time to study their briefs, sometimes not even time to read them, let alone think out the problems facing the movement.

This would not matter so much if they could rely on an army

of experts to do their thinking for them as can a Government Minister, or a top business executive, or an American trade union leader. But the very fact that they are paid such low salaries precludes this. If they were to pay the 'rate for the job' to economists, or lawyers, or industrial efficiency engineers, or public relations officers, these men would in many cases be earning far more than the general secretaries and the basis of the staff salary structure would be upset. Two of the biggest unions have given as one reason for not appointing a press officer that they cannot pay the salary that would be expected by a London journalist. Consequently many union leaders remain without the expert assistance they need or else rely on amateur 'experts'.

District officers, themselves overburdened, often complain that general secretaries do not give enough time to their own union.

There is an able group of young men in charge of the various departments of the T.U.C. at Congress House but most remain there only because they are willing to make a substantial financial sacrifice. The rate of turnover among the assistants is high. This is particularly true of the research department, which lost all its six members in three years, but the social insurance and production departments have also lost staff.

The refusal of unions to pay their officials the rate for the job is one aspect of the determination of members to have unionism on the cheap. Perhaps the rank and file feel that they are not getting the service from their leaders that they ought to have. Union dues have not nearly kept pace with the rise in earnings or in the cost of living since the war; still less have they been increased to provide for increased union responsibilities.

The T.U.C. General Council have for some time been worried about the financial position of the unions. In 1955 and 1956 they conducted a survey which showed that while workers' earnings had trebled since before the war, union contributions had risen by about a quarter – from an average of 11d. to 1s. 2d. Yet costs of administration per member had risen about eighty per cent and nearly fifty-eight unions spent more than they received in contributions.

Some unions said that because of their restricted finances they could not give the services demanded by members. The development of such activities as recruitment, propaganda, education, and the training of officers was being hampered. One said that the salaries they could offer were not enough to attract first-class officers and that in consequence the standard of district officials was deteriorating. Among reasons given for the refusal of members to agree to increased contributions was the fear of competition for membership, a feeling that expenses should be cut first, and the suggestion that reserves should be used up first.

Some union contributions were raised after that, but other proposed increases were turned down, and the T.U.C. remained uneasy. In 1959 they said that many unions could not afford to train their officers and members in modern management and technical methods, and doubted whether training was being given to more than 1000 officers a year of the many thousands involved in negotiations arising out of new management techniques and incentive schemes.

They made a new survey and in 1960 reported little improvement. The number of unions spending more than their contribution income had risen to 75 out of the 125 surveyed. The proportion of basic wage rates paid as union subscriptions, while fractionally up, was still only about $\frac{3}{4}$ of 1 per cent, compared with about $1\frac{1}{2}$ per cent in 1939.

The T.U.C. itself has always been kept short of money. Its income in 1959 was a little over £320,000, of which £63,000 went in international affiliation fees and £86,000 to educational and other grants and the Congress House building fund.

Low salaries at the top mean low salaries all the way down the trade union hierarchy. Local officials often earn less than many of the workers they represent, so that a trade union career has ceased to be attractive. They have too much to do and hardly any expert advice. Many observers have formed the impression that the calibre of trade union leadership at area and district level has deteriorated as their responsibilities have increased. Many are so burdened it is almost impossible for them to do a good job. Mr Ben Roberts has estimated that American unions have about one paid employee for every 300 members while the British have about one for every 900 members.

The impression that the quality of district officials has deteriorated is not capable of proof, but there have certainly been occasions when no outstanding candidate has been available for higher union offices when they fell vacant. One reason for the success of Communist candidates in a few unions is that they are often men of greater ability than their opponents. Dedicated to a cause, they are less discouraged by low rates of pay.

Another important factor is that the brightest boys from working-class households often do not enter the ranks of manual workers at all. The modern educational system provides opportunities which skim off the cream of the younger generation to turn them into technicians or black-coated workers of one sort or another. Against this, improvements in the level of education should produce new generations of workers with better trained minds.

At the same time greater demands are made upon the official. He has to deal with workers and their army of shop stewards and other unpaid officers who have the independence that comes from good wages and security. He has to know something of modern industrial techniques, work study, complicated incentive schemes, not to mention general economics, and the financial position of the industry and the individual firms with which he deals.

Trade union education has been expanded to train officials to do their job more efficiently. Between 1948 and 1958, annual T.U.C. expenditure increased from £7000 to £35,000 and the expenditure of individual unions from £50,400 to £244,250. It is still not nearly enough. Some eighty or ninety of the smaller unions still provide no educational facilities at all. Many do not even take advantage of the free openings provided under the T.U.C. training scheme.

Moreover the best use is not made of the money spent because of overlapping and competition between the organizations providing facilities. There was a split in workers' education more than half a century ago and it has never been healed. The National Council of Labour Colleges and the Workers' Educational Trade Union Committee, associated with the Workers' Educational Association, continue to compete for pupils throughout the country, while the T.U.C., the individual unions, and Ruskin College all have their own schemes and some of the university

extra-mural departments have also entered the field on a substantial scale. In 1948 the General Council examined the possibility of rationalizing trade union education and gave it up as
hopeless. In 1959 they made a fresh survey and were working on
a definite plan in 1961. Apart from rationalizing the present
education services, the useful suggestion has been made that
branches should be encouraged to appoint education officers.

There are still able men who embark on a trade union career
because it satisfies a desire to serve their fellow-men or because
it is a relatively easy road to power, but there are too few of them.
The picture as a whole is of divided, overworked, and underpaid
national leaders, without adequate expert advice, and of a proportion of under-equipped mediocrities at the lower levels. The
result has been hesitant and unimaginative leadership, slow to
come to grips with the deficiencies which will be discussed in the
ensuing chapters.

2

A PLANLESS SOCIETY

Include Us Out – Drifting Up the Spiral – Busmen's Battle –
Rattlesnake Pie – Proud Empiricists

The more it becomes a feature of the trade unions' policy to
advocate changes in the nation's industrial and social relation-
ships, the more is it incumbent on the trade unions to envisage
the part to be played by them in that changed environment. It
little becomes those who would seek to substitute for natural
forces a greater degree of conscious control even to appear to
assume that consequential changes in their own outlook and struc-
ture either will be unnecessary or must be left to develop naturally—
Alan Birch (now chairman of the T.U.C. economic committee)
in his paper on *Structure of the British Trade Union Movement*
(see Preface.)

The T.U.C. constantly declare their belief in planning the
national economy yet they have not planned for their own
movement. The big unions all have their independent policies,
often in competition and conflict with each other. The structure
of the movement is as haphazard (as will be described in
Chapter 4), as its policy is confused. Little is done to put either
in order.

This is not because the T.U.C. are unaware that changes are
needed. It is because they have not the power to carry them out.
The individual unions insist on their own autonomy. They may
surrender some aspects of policy-making to federations or other
joint bodies in particular industries. The engineering and shipbuilding and the building unions, for instance, adopt common
policies on basic wages and conditions. But they will not
surrender them to the T.U.C.

The T.U.C. General Council have, indeed, considerable powers,
but they are primarily concerned with union conduct and inter-
union disputes. On broad matters of policy they have only a

moral influence. Whatever resolutions may be passed by congresses, individual unions remain free to go their own way. When the T.U.C. tried to establish agreed policies on wages and productivity, during the period of the Labour Government, they adopted the device of calling conferences of union executives, but such conferences could only increase the moral effect of the decisions taken. They could not and did not bind the unions.

This weakness of the T.U.C. has damaged the movement in the post-war period because for most of the time it has made a rational wages policy impossible. The failure of the movement to tackle the wages issue is indeed its most serious weakness, much more serious than official or unofficial strikes, demarcation disputes, closed shops, election abuses, or any of the other things about which the public has been justifiably disturbed.

The unions have always insisted that wages should not be planned by the Government and they have failed to agree on any way of coordinating their wages policy themselves. The instinctive reaction of most trade unionists to the words 'national wages policy' in a resolution is to move 'next business'. The result in the period of full employment since the war has been continual competition in wage claims, leapfrogging over each other in a never-ending inflationary succession. Even within some single industries, like the railways, the unions have frequently been unable to agree on a common policy.

That sort of thing makes obvious nonsense of talk about a planned economy. One would not wish to criticize the T.U.C. for having failed to solve the problem of wages under full employment. It has not been satisfactorily solved in any other free country and no one in this country really knows the answer. But since 1950 they have given up the attempt to find an answer. If no answer is found, the only way of dealing with the inflationary spiral is that adopted by the Conservative Government – monetary and financial restrictions followed by some unemployment and periods of industrial stagnation. Wage restraint under the Labour Government was a temporary palliative which broke down. In short, the failure of the unions to find a reasonable wage policy made continuous full employment impossible.

The problem is by now familiar to most people. Full employment greatly strengthens the negotiating power of the unions. Wage rates are forced up. Because labour is scarce, employers offer inducements to attract workers from their competitors, so earnings rise faster still. Because wages rise faster than production, prices rise, rapidly swallowing up the gains in wages and provoking new claims. Competition between employers may take the form either of bonuses and premiums, unnecessary overtime, and slack piece rates, or of fringe benefits, such as pension schemes, sickness pay and so on. Often they retain on their pay roll scarce workers they do not need at the time, lest they suffer from a shortage later on.

The T.U.C. General Council foresaw during the war that they would be faced with this problem. In their interim report on post-war reconstruction in 1944 they said that a policy of full employment would impose obligations on the workers and that a disciplined observance of collective agreements and a higher degree of mobility of labour between occupations would be necessary. 'Provided the Government was able to give adequate guarantees that it was genuinely pursuing a policy of full employment and was determined to take all necessary steps to control prices and otherwise prevent the exploitation of the situation by private interests,' the report continued, 'the trades unions would undertake to avoid wage policies and demarcation and other practices which might impede the achievement of full employment'.

One could wish that the T.U.C. would re-examine their industrial policy today with as much foresight as they showed then. During the period of the Labour Government, they tried valiantly to carry out their undertakings. The Government in 1947 were anxious to secure restraint in wage claims on the part of unions generally but to allow increases in certain vital, undermanned industries such as coal and cotton so as to attract labour to them without workers in other industries insisting that the existing differentials should be preserved.

Arthur Deakin would have nothing to do with the latter part of this plan, which might have worked to the disadvantage of many of his members. In no circumstances, he declared at the 1947 Labour Party conference, would they accept the position that responsibility for fixing of wages and regulation of conditions of employment was one for the Government. As an alternative, he used his influence to induce the trade union movement to accept the reintroduction of a limited direction of labour to increase recruitment to undermanned industries.

The economic crises that year resulted in long discussion between the Government and the T.U.C., who appealed to the unions to use 'even greater moderation' than before, but wage claims continued. The Government persevered, however, and in 1948 produced a statement on 'Personal Incomes, Costs, and Prices' which advanced further than any British Government had previously gone in peace-time towards a wages policy. Pointing to the dangers of inflation, the statement said there should be no further increase in the level of personal incomes without a corresponding increase in the volume of production.

While reiterating that it was undesirable for the Government to interfere directly with the incomes of individuals, except by taxation, the statement said it was essential that there should be strict adherence to the terms of collective agreements, as departures from agreed conditions by individual employers might lead to competitive bargaining, that there was no justification for any general increase of money incomes, but that there might be cases in which increases in wages or salaries would be justified from a national point of view to attract workers to undermanned industries. A marked rise in the cost of living would make it necessary to reconsider personal incomes which became inadequate.

The union leaders, faced with this declaration of policy without prior consultation, were at first doubtful if they could get the support of their members, but eventually they accepted the statement with five modifications which considerably weakened its force. They referred for instance to 'the necessity of adjusting the wages of those whose incomes are below a reasonable standard of subsistence' and 'the need to safeguard those wage differentials which are an essential element in the wages structure of many important industries'. There were ample loopholes for those unions which opposed the policy to justify new wage claims.

A new economic crisis in 1949, accompanied by devaluation of the £, was followed by a Government appeal for something more than the existing policy of restraint. All kinds of possibilities were discussed. The Government offered to introduce a statutory minimum wage to make sure that no workers fell below a minimum standard of life. Some form of coordinating authority was suggested to decide whether new claims were justified in the national interest.

Both were rejected because of union insistence that there should be no outside interference with their freedom. Eventually, however, the General Council did arrive at proposals which were remarkable evidence of their anxiety to help. They suggested that all unions should reconsider their existing wage claims, that unions with sliding scales relating wages to the cost of living (covering some 2,500,000 workers) should suspend them, and that claims should not be pressed unless the price index rose by more than five points. At the same time the General Council announced that they would intensify the campaign they were carrying on for higher productivity.

It was more than their members would stand. The proposals were carried by a narrow majority at a conference of union executives but the unions with sliding scales refused to suspend them, the engineers and railwaymen continued to press their claims, and the miners and distribution workers reversed their executives' support for the new policy.

In June 1950, the General Council issued a new statement of policy accepting the need for greater flexibility but by then reaction against the scheme had gone too far. At the congress in September the General Council were defeated, albeit narrowly, on a resolution calling on them to abandon the policy of wage restraint.

That was the end of the T.U.C.'s efforts to carry through a wages policy. The shock of defeat was too much for them. Whether they would have revived the attempt if Labour had remained in office is a matter for surmise. In September 1951, Mr Gaitskell, as Chancellor of the Exchequer, was once more trying to secure trade union cooperation to keep down wages, offering as inducements temporary legal limitation of dividends, extended controls, a stronger monopolies commission, the prohibition of resale price maintenance, and even, if necessary, some increase in subsidies. However, Labour lost office before bargaining could begin.

The Conservative Governments which followed relied mainly on monetary measures to restrain inflation, but they also, particularly at first, made appeals to the unions. In 1952 the Congress accepted a statement from the General Council which contained a warning about the danger of wage increases which would increase the price of exports, but added that it did not follow that wage earners were not justified in seeking wage increases. It did not appear that this had the slightest effect on big claims being pressed at that time.

Government warnings were renewed in succeeding years and with increased urgency in 1955. The T.U.C., while still recognizing the dangers, and rejecting motions advocating that all restraint should be cast aside, had no positive policy to put forward. In a Budget statement the following year they were still saying: 'The lesson which every working-class family has learned over the past fifteen years is that increases in wages have largely been cancelled out by increases in prices. This process will continue unless rises in incomes are kept broadly in line with increases in output or until it is terminated by unemployment.'

But in September 1956, Congress finally threw off the last trace of wage restraint. The Prime Minister, Sir Anthony Eden, had a series of meetings with representatives of the T.U.C. and employers' organizations and finally again urged restraint in wages, profits, and dividends to keep prices steady. The reply of Congress, in a resolution moved by Mr Cousins, was: 'This Congress recognizes the critical weakness of the national economy and places a large measure of responsibility for recent inflationary trends on the Government's failure after 1951 to maintain and improve the export trade. By abandoning economic controls on the plea of setting the people free, the Government left the economy to drift and deprived themselves of the most effective means of recovering control in a crisis. Congress asserts the right of labour to bargain on equal terms with capital, and to use its bargaining strength to protect the workers from the dislocations of an unplanned economy. It rejects proposals to recover control by wage restraint and by using the nationalized industries as a drag-anchor for the drifting national economy.' Similar resolutions rejecting restraint have been passed at every succeeding Congress.

In a sense, the union attitude towards appeals by a Conservative Government has been understandable. They were united in believing that the Government's policy was misguided and that it imposed a disproportionate burden on the workers. They were opposed to the removal of controls and subsidies which led to rising prices when imports were becoming cheaper. They were opposed to the method of meeting inflation by financial restrictions which, in their view, halted the increase in production and produced increased unemployment from 1958–9. Since the Government had reintroduced the law of the jungle, they said, their only course was to fight for what they could get. The Government, they said in a long statement on economic policy in the summer of 1959, had made price stability rather than full employment their prime objective, and had placed the main burden on the shoulders of the workers.

'Trade unionists', the statement went on, 'are entitled to expect that any Government will do everything it can to maintain full employment and improve living standards, and any Government that is genuinely and consistently seeking to promote those ends is entitled to demand and to get the cooperation of all sections of the community, including the trade union movement. Trade unionists cannot themselves determine the nation's economic policies, but they are bound to react to the conditions created by those policies. When attempts are made to throw on to trade unionists responsibility for the Government's own failures, hostile reactions from trade unionists must be expected, but the movement has shown its readiness to respond to the challenge of advance and opportunity.'

This shifting of the blame on to the Government seemed to the movement's critics an abdication of responsibility. The union leaders were well aware that it was in large measure the constant

41

pressure of wage increases on prices which forced the Government to impose the economic restrictions they so disliked.

'The condition of reasonable price stability is that the increase in incomes should keep step with the growth of real output – not that output should be restricted in an attempt to prevent the growth of incomes,' they said. But it was partly because increases in wages had gone ahead of the growth of output that the Government had felt obliged to take the measures which restricted output.

Yet another passage in the report largely accepts this: 'Difficulties can arise from the facts that, unless rises in incomes are matched by greater output, the tendency is to drive up prices and that, while each group of income earners may be aware that any further general rise in incomes would be frustrated by a corresponding rise in prices, its anxiety to maintain its own position relative to other sections spurs it on to demand higher incomes. No Government could by itself guarantee that full employment would be accompanied by price stability unless it adopted totalitarian methods of controlling production and the movement of labour and fixing incomes. But, as was said earlier, a Government which is genuinely and consistently seeking to maintain full employment and improve living standards, and whose policies are seen to be socially and economically equitable, can reasonably expect trade unionists to cooperate in avoiding difficulties of this sort.' That was in effect a reiteration of their undertaking to cooperate with a new Labour Government if it adopted policies which they advocated. And it was as far as they ever went.

They have never attempted to work out in any detail a wage policy for the next period of Labour Government which would avoid the strains, stresses, and failures of the 1945–51 period. They are not doing so now. They cannot do so, because they refuse to accept a central policy, and cooperation with a Government is impossible without a central policy.

Had Labour won in 1959, the results of this attitude might well have been lamentable. But just as lamentable is the unions' refusal even to attempt a reasonable policy under a Conservative Government. They simply wash their hands of the situation described in their report, where different groups compete for wage increases which are offset by price increases. If they cannot work with the Government, one might have thought they would try to get together to make the best of it, instead of competing against each other – in other words that they would have tried to work out a trade union wage policy.

There has, indeed, been talk of coordination of policy. Mr Birch, in his paper quoted at the beginning of this chapter, said that most of the problems which are likely to confront the unions with increasing intensity are such as to be incapable of solution within the individual unions themselves. They involve relationships with each other and the adoption of a common policy towards many of the issues which hitherto have been dealt with individually. The T.U.C.'s inability to give any pledges on behalf of the trade union movement, he further argued, reduces their power to influence Government economic policy.

To criticisms that national consideration of wages policy in individual industries would bring the whole weight of the movement behind every application, Mr Birch replied that coordination would not involve any interference with the collective bargaining machinery in each industry, but it would tend to eliminate competing and sometimes irreconcilable claims. For the T.U.C. to share in the determination of wages policy would reduce rather than widen the gulf between union leaders and rank and file, and supplementary negotiations at factory or shop level would become of even greater importance than now.

Coordination of policy has also been advocated, for quite different reasons, by men like Mr Frank Foulkes, the Communist, who want alliances to force up wages more rapidly still. Such talk was given impetus by the London bus strike of 1958.

Nearly every year there is some resolution at Congress advocating a national or coordinated wage policy, but it never gets far. In 1955, Mr Geddes (as he was then) gave a presidential address to Congress in which he advocated an economic survey of the post-war years followed by a special conference of executives to formulate a national trade union economic policy. A survey followed four years later but the idea of a special conference of executives has not been heard of again.

In 1957 a resolution moved by the National Union of Tailors

and Garment Workers, suggesting the establishment of a new department to provide information on wages and closer association between the General Council and all the affiliated organizations on related wage questions, was easily defeated. But the London bus strike forced the union leaders to look at the problem seriously.

Most of the union leaders felt that the London busmen were fighting a test case against the Government's policy of keeping down wages in the public sector of industry and other forms of public employment, and indeed against the Government's wage policy generally. They accepted the position that there is a pattern in each round of wage settlements which is set by those unions which take the initiative and bear the brunt of the struggle. But it was widely felt that the bus strike was badly handled and that it was the wrong industry to act as a spearhead. The absence of buses irritated the public without exerting much economic pressure on anybody. Moreover the General Council, while they gave the strike verbal support and encouraged financial help, could not increase the pressure without a direct clash with the Government, which would have been disastrous for the movement. Defeat was inevitable.

The leaders of the movement were deeply disturbed and began to consider whether in future they should not marshal their forces better and choose their own ground for a struggle. In September that year the Congress passed without opposition a resolution from the Fire Brigades Union instructing the General Council 'to examine whether further progress can be made to meet the urgent need of greater coordination in the policies and activities of unions with related interests.'

The General Council's report in 1959 on the Fire Brigades' resolution was almost entirely negative. They said that further progress towards closer working between unions was indeed needed, and that in industries where several unions were involved there were or should be procedures for one union to notify the others about a pay claim it was going to make. 'The fraternal spirit of trade unionism demands that unions shall help each other when in difficulties: it also demands that those whose help will be expected shall be informed beforehand of the circumstances and be given an opportunity of reaching prior agreement on the steps to be taken to conclude mutually accepted and coordinated policies.' But they found no evidence that delegate conferences and executive committees of unions wished to relinquish or modify substantially their rights of decision about wages.

The Congress approved this but at the same time, with characteristic lack of logic, approved a resolution from the Union of Shop, Distributive and Allied Workers vaguely advocating an inquiry into the possibility of greater coordination. Mr Birch, who moved the resolution, actually said that he agreed entirely with the logic of the report, negative though the recommendations might seem.

What Mr Birch had in mind in moving the resolution, as he explained, was that unions should consult with the General Council on industrial policy before their annual conferences. 'Would this help', he asked, 'to lead to wider considerations being injected into those conference discussions, to a greater degree of coordination in the timing of wages claims, and a better appreciation of the relationship of those wages claims to Congress policy as a whole?'

This was very like what Mr Foulkes had been saying a year earlier, yet Mr Foulkes opposed the resolution, presumably because he suspected its object was to restrain inflationary wage claims. He said he was in favour of union cooperation to force wages up but against union cooperation to keep them down. The resolution was also opposed by Mr Douglas, on the extreme right, apparently because he feared Mr Birch had a planned wages policy in mind, in spite of Mr Birch's denials. It was also opposed by men like Mr Carron, of the Amalgamated Engineering Union, because they feared it would play into the hands of Mr Foulkes and the Communists in their attempts to mass the strength of the unions for major struggles.

Mr Foulkes was president of the Confederation of Shipbuilding and Engineering Unions that year and that position, combined with his office as president of the Electrical Trades Union, enabled him to try and get some practical coordination of policy, particularly on the forty-hour week, which was being given priority over wages in the minds of most union leaders. Claims for a shorter week had been turned down in most industries for several years in succession.

The trade union side of the national joint council for the electricity supply industry, of which Mr Foulkes was also chairman, approached the Confederation with a view to coordinating their policy and later there were talks with the miners' leaders, whose claim for a shorter week had been rejected and who were considering arbitration. As a result, the miners held their hands. It was agreed that the engineering unions should act as the spearhead, for both wages and hours, in the private sector of industry, and the electricity supply unions for hours in the public sector. With its high profits and low labour costs, the electricity supply industry was demonstrably the weak link among the nationalized industries.

There were some suggestions at the 1959 Congress that the T.U.C. should act on behalf of the whole movement on shorter hours, but this was not acceptable. The General Council were instructed, however, to inform the Government and industry of their intention, with affiliated unions, to reduce the weekly hours of labour. Later in the year they issued a statement saying that the time had come for a shorter working week, but in the meantime a forty-two-hour week had been negotiated in one or two industries, and seemed certain to spread to others, so that the T.U.C.'s action made no material difference.

Another issue which was raised by the London bus strike in an acute form was the method of fixing the pay of workers in nationalized industries or other public employment. In the autumn of 1957 the Government imposed a number of monetary and economic restrictions. At the same time, they said they were not prepared to finance inflationary wage increases, mentioning particularly the British Transport Commission. Increases in the Civil Service, however obtained, would have to be met by compensatory economies, even if that meant reductions in staff. They appealed to all concerned, including 'those who adjudicate about wages', to bear the dangers of inflation in mind.

This advice to those who adjudicate about wages was taken as an instruction to arbitration tribunals and greatly incensed the unions. Some declared they would not in future accept arbitration.

In the operation of their policy, the Government disallowed a pay increase for health service staff which had been agreed upon by the Whitley Council. They similarly rejected a settlement for firewomen's pay. They made some reductions in staff where increases in pay in sections of the Civil Service were obtained by arbitration. The trade unions concerned and the T.U.C. protested vigorously. The health service employees imposed an overtime ban.

But the differences really came to a head with the bus dispute. The unions, no doubt rightly, held the Government responsible for the rejection of the busmen's claim by the London Transport Executive. 'Government policy has brought London's buses to a standstill,' declared the T.U.C. General Council on 7 May 1958. 'Having mismanaged the economy, the Government has chosen the pay claim of London's busmen as an opportunity to put pressure on a public employer to conform to its policy of holding down wages, and to bolster the resistance of private employers in whose negotiations with unions it cannot directly interfere.' As has been recalled, the General Council later declined to go so far as to authorize the extension of the strike, but their attitude to the Government's policy remained bitter.

The trouble then arose because the Government were doing their utmost to prevent wage increases, but on other occasions they have been severely criticized for bringing pressure on nationalization boards to concede increases, particularly on railwaymen, rather than plunge the country into damaging strikes. Once or twice this has meant overruling an arbitration award. Private employers have expressed resentment, blaming the Government in such circumstances for starting a round of inflationary wage increases.

The position of Government conciliators, when the Government has adopted so active a wages policy, has been made extremely difficult. The question has been raised whether the function of conciliation would not be better undertaken by an independent authority.

An import development in the fixing of wages in publicly owned industries was the setting up of the Guillebaud committee to compare wages on the railways with those in outside industry. Railway wages were revised on the basis of their report in 1960; the principle was similar to that adopted in the Civil Service, where pay is based on 'fair comparison' with pay outside after investigations have been made by the Civil Service Pay Research Unit.

The T.U.C. presented a report on 'Government interference in nationalized industries' to the 1960 Congress, after obtaining the views of the unions concerned. There was no agreement, they said, on whether it would be possible or desirable for Ministers to take up an attitude of neutrality to wage claims in these industries and services, but there was some support for the suggestion that it would be helpful if fair comparisons with other industries could be established independently.

The General Council agreed that the method of fair comparison would decrease the possibility of unions meeting the Government in head-on collision about wages and should reduce the effects of Government and ministerial interference. Moreover, they pointed out, it would provide a standard by which wages in these industries could be adjusted without running into the criticism that increased charges were exploiting the public.

On the other hand, they thought it could lead to unions playing a less enterprising role in the industries concerned and there was the practical point that any extension of nationalization would diminish the area from which comparisons could be drawn. It could also be argued, they pointed out, that an automatic mechanism removed a necessary element of flexibility from the economy.

On balance, they considered that the objections to accepting the comparative method were strong, but that this did not impair its value for special cases. Raising wages in a depressed section by this method, however, would be of no benefit if other unions demanded consequential increases.

Finally the General Council became enmeshed in one of their most turgid series of almost meaningless generalizations. What mattered, perhaps, was their view that public ownership could hardly operate without some degree of ministerial control – in other words interference – and that if this adversely affected the work-people, then the unions must insist on their freedom to protect their members without being accused of using industrial action for political purposes or directing it irresponsibly against the community.

In other words, in spite of the warning of 1958, things must be left as they are and unions must have freedom to fight the Government if they think it necessary.

An obscure aspect of T.U.C. policy is their attitude towards workers' participation in the control of industry. The interim report on post-war reconstruction in 1944 listed three main trade union objectives. The first two were full employment and improved living standards.

The third objective was described as follows: 'The trade union movement exists to extend the influence of work-people over the policies and purposes of industry and to arrange for their participation in its management. The claim to share in the control of industry rests primarily on the simple democratic right of work-people to have a voice in the determination of their industrial destinies. It is supported by the knowledge that it is only by recognition of this claim that the potentialities, experience, and good sense of the workers can be drawn upon and the full productive powers of industry be effectively realized.'

The economic report in 1959 listed only two objectives of the trade union movement's economic policy – full employment and improved living standards. Workers' participation is not even mentioned in a list of secondary objectives and so has presumably been dropped or relegated to a minor position. There has been no formal decision to make this change and probably most trade unionists are unaware that it has happened. There has for some time, however, been evidence that the movement has been growing lukewarm.

There have been advocates of workers' control of industry throughout the history of the movement, from Robert Owen at the beginning of the nineteenth century to Tom Mann and the Guild Socialists nearly a century later. What was in mind in

1944, however, was something different – not control but participation in control through cooperation with employers at every
level of the economy, national and local. There was to be a
national industrial council, consultative councils for nationalized
industries, industrial boards for private industries, regional
boards, and district committees.

Many joint bodies had already been set up during the war, and
after it the Labour Government took pains to develop the idea.
They did not, it is true, establish a national industrial council,
but there were the economic planning board, with both sides
represented, and numerous joint advisory bodies including the
National Joint Advisory Council, the National Production
Advisory Council on Industry, regional boards, and committees.
Some development councils were established and one or two
joint advisory councils for particular industries. Joint consultative councils and committees were obligatory in nationalized
industries at all levels and actively encouraged in private firms.
The British Productivity Council was created to encourage
improved productivity.

After the Conservatives were returned to power, the two or
three existing development councils were dispensed with. The
rest of the structure was maintained, but with steadily declining
vitality. In the face of this, the trade union attitude has been
contradictory. The 1952 Congress rejected a proposal to enforce
joint consultation by legislation. The T.U.C. production committee has continued active interest in the bodies on which the
General Council is represented, has pressed for the inclusion of
trade union representatives in research organizations, and in 1959
proposed that the N.P.A.C.I. should be used more purposefully.

The T.U.C. also conducted a leisurely survey of joint consultation in the various nationalized industries (where it is compulsory), generally seeming to find little or nothing that could be
improved. Neither at trade union conferences nor at the Congress,
however, has there been any evidence of interest in the subject.

'Our own union', said a writer in the *Railway Review* in 1959,
'presumably is still bound by the 1948 Annual General Meeting
decision of participating in the management of industry. But we
have, in common with other similarly situated unions, done little

or nothing to convince the movement of the correctness of this conception of the future. Indeed, rattlesnake pie would be as popular in some sections of our movement as this once held general concept of our historical role.'

Mr Hugh Gaitskell's original draft for the new statement of objects of the Labour Party in 1960 contained a reference to the right of the workers 'to full consultation and participation in all the vital decisions of management'. The words 'and participation' were cut out before the statement reached its final form.

The preoccupation is with conflict, not collaboration. While workers' participation has apparently been dropped as a primary aim of the movement, there has been no discussion of the change and no attempt to consider its implications. The old arrangements have been running down and there is no new impetus. The kind of industrial society which the movement then sought was carefully described in 1944. Now, apparently, it cares only for full employment and more money and leisure.

A particularly glaring example of the movement's failure to think ahead was its attitude to redundancy of workers. During all the years of full employment neither the T.U.C. nor most of the unions (except in nationalized industries) made any attempt to develop a redundancy policy and negotiate agreements with the employers, though favourable agreements could probably have been had almost for the asking at that time. Then, when a recession came, they found themselves obliged to do what they could for their members in difficult circumstances.

Even now, there can be no generally agreed policy because the Amalgamated Engineering Union, supported by some others, insists that all redundancy must be opposed, even though their own leaders know this to be unrealistic. A few fairly good agreements have been made here and there, but on the whole displaced workers leave their employment on much less favourable terms, in respect of length of notice, compensation, and so on, than could have been obtained for them by far-sighted leaders.

The trade union attitude to strikes and arbitration is also somewhat obscure. We are concerned here with official strikes, as unofficial strikes, which sometimes present different issues, will be discussed in a later chapter.

The wartime prohibition of strikes and provison for compulsory binding arbitration under the National Arbitration Order was continued by agreement until 1951. Unofficial strikes took place, generally with impunity. After legal proceedings had been taken against certain unofficial strikers, however, the T.U.C. asked for a change. The result was the Industrial Disputes Order, which legalized strikes (and lock-outs) but retained provision for either side to report a dispute to the Minister of Labour for reference to the Industrial Disputes Tribunal, the awards of which became an implied term of contract enforceable in the courts.

In 1954 Sir Godfrey Ince, then Permanent Secretary to the Minister of Labour, suggested that negotiating machinery in all industries should make provision for settling disputes by arbitration if necessary. The National Joint Advisory Council discussed this but the T.U.C. pointed out that some industries with successful records in negotiation had no provision for arbitration while some which made provision for arbitration had bad records. It was agreed that the possibility might be drawn to the attention of some industries, but that was all.

After they were made legal again, official strikes continued rare, but in 1955 there were three in succession, in the newspaper, dock, and railway industries, all of which arose partly or mainly out of rivalry between unions. Public opinion was disturbed. Such a series of official strikes had not been known for a generation. It was widely felt that national strikes were outdated in a period when the economy was constantly under strain.

There was a debate in the House of Commons at which numerous suggestions were put forward. They included the setting up of a 'Parliament of Industry' or 'national economic council', legislation to enforce secret ballots of union members before strikes are called, the setting up of an independent commission to investigate the subject, a voluntary period of reflection before strike notices are issued, the development of profit-sharing and copartnership, improvements in joint consultation and human relations, voluntary extension of arbitration procedure, stopping income tax refunds to strikers and public assistance to their families, improvement of procedure for handling inter-union disputes.

The Minister of Labour (Mr Macleod) said he attached great importance to a period of reflection and consideration before getting into an atmosphere of strikes and strike notices. 'Indeed,' he added, 'I think myself that it is very desirable that we should consider, no doubt with the British Employers' Confederation and the Trades Union Congress, whether we cannot try to secure a period of reflection whenever it is possible to do so.'

However, he does not seem to have pressed that particularly hard in the discussions that followed. The Prime Minister (Sir Anthony Eden) had talks with the unions, employers, and nationalized industries. The Minister of Labour asked the members of the National Joint Advisory Council to consider the various suggestions made in the House, and there was a long series of fruitless meetings.

The General Council, who had played a part in the settlement of the strikes, recognized that the T.U.C. had to accept some responsibility in so far as the strikes were the result of inter-union rivalry. They already had power to intervene, when negotiations reached a deadlock of such a character as to involve other bodies of workers or to imperil standard wages or hours and conditions of employment, by calling representatives of the organizations into consultation and using their influence to effect a settlement. Their reaction now was to ask Congress for power to intervene in a dispute before deadlock had been reached.

Modest as this proposal might seem, unions representing more than three million workers voted against it. There could hardly be stronger evidence than this of the extreme reluctance of the unions to increase the authority of the T.U.C.

Some critics of the unions who accept the inevitability of strikes are nevertheless opposed to their extension by sympathetic action or 'secondary boycotts', as they are called in the United States. Both official and unofficial strikes may be extended in various ways to those not directly involved in the dispute, either in the same union or in other unions.

The most famous example of this was the General Strike of 1926, when a large proportion of the country's workers came out in support of the miners. Earlier still, the triple alliance of miners, railwaymen, and transport workers attempted to put sympathetic action on a systematic basis by promising to support each other.

The crisis in the London bus strike of 1958 came when Mr Cousins threatened to extend it to petrol and power workers. The National Union of Railwaymen, in more than one crisis over general railway pay, have threatened to call out underground workers and railway shopmen not actually in dispute.

More common than straightforward support are the disputes which arise from refusal to handle 'black' goods. In the B.M.C. redundancy strike of 1956, the Transport and General Workers' Union ordered dockers and lorry drivers to refuse to touch B.M.C. products, bus drivers not to carry men to work, and building trade members not to engage on B.M.C. construction and repairs, while the Amalgamated Engineering Union instructed its members throughout the engineering industry to refuse to work on accessories for the corporation, and the National Union of Railwayman ordered their members not to carry B.M.C. products.

The strike of 1700 meat transport drivers in 1958 first spread to Smithfield market, which was brought to a standstill, and then to the docks, stopping work over the greater part of the Port of London. Journalists were involved in the 1959 printing strike because they were instructed to refuse to work for 'black' newspapers.

In the dispute between D. C. Thomson and Company, the Scottish newspaper proprietors, and the National Society of Operative Printers and Assistants in 1952, over non-unionism, the T.U.C. issued more than a million copies of a statement asking trade unionists not to buy the firm's publications. The Printing and Kindred Trades Federation appealed to their member unions to take direct action and to outside unions to prevent the firm from receiving materials or distributing their product. As a result disputes arose in the paper-making and newspaper distribution industries.

If workers in the transport industry responded to every appeal not to carry black goods, they would seldom work. Apart from frequent unofficial action by the dockers, they carry on with their normal work except in special circumstances. Dock strikes rapidly spread from port to port as ships are diverted.

But little or no thought has been given to the general principles which should guide unions in these matters.

The union attitude to arbitration is particularly incoherent. In recent years, big unions have again and again attacked the arbitration machinery and refused offers by employers to settle disputes by arbitration. This happened particularly frequently after 1957 when the Government gave their famous advice to those who adjudicate on wages to bear the dangers of inflation in mind.

At one time or another, the engineers and shipbuilders, railwaymen, printers, sections of the transport workers, and others have refused to go to arbitration, contending that the tribunals were influenced by Government policy and that the employers were trying to make offers of arbitration an excuse for refusing to negotiate. In 1957, when a dispute over the pay of provincial busmen was referred to the Industrial Disputes Tribunal, the unions announced beforehand that they would not cooperate in the hearings and would not be bound by the award. (In the event, the award was so favourable that they accepted it.)

It was not surprising that the following year, when the Government announced their intention to terminate the Industrial Disputes Order, the employers asked for the compulsory element in arbitration procedure to be brought to an end. But unions which had been attacking arbitration for years immediately became righteously indignant.

The apparent lack of logic in this is readily explicable. While strongly organized workers might prefer to rely on strikes or threats of strikes, there were many weaker groups of peaceful-minded workers, particularly white-collar workers like the local government officers, who had regularly resorted to the I.D.T. The employers argued reasonably that they could not expect to have it both ways. Compulsory arbitration came to an end, but the provision in the order to compel individual employers to adopt recognized terms and conditions was preserved in the Terms and Conditions of Employment Act, 1959.

Union policy now seems to be to restore compulsory arbitration, presumably with the strong unions maintaining their refusal to accept it.

The broad position is that nearly seventy industries are known to contain provision for arbitration in their agreements, but comparatively few provide that the arbitration shall be binding. Apart from the nationalized industries already mentioned, these few include textile finishing, oil distribution, paint, varnish, and lacquer manufacture, cement, electrical cable making, and motor vehicle retail and repairing. Nearly eighty industries are known not to mention arbitration in their agreements, though many of them resort to it if necessary.

We have referred in this chapter to some of the major issues on which trade union policy is inadequate or confused. Others could have been mentioned. The movement seems to have lost the capacity to take a broad view of itself and its problems or to plan for the future. Making a virtue of necessity, some of its leaders pride themselves on their purely empiric approach.

3

A PRIVATE PARTY

THERE is no aspect of policy towards which the trade union
attitude has seemed more confused than Socialism. The trade
unions were largely responsible for the creation in 1900 of the
Labour Representation Committee which became the Labour
Party in 1906. Though the party was formed in association with
the Independent Labour Party and other Socialist organizations,
most trade union leaders at that time were Liberals and the
Labour Party did not at first include the establishment of a
Socialist state among its aims.

The period before the First World War saw the rapid growth
of Socialist societies and the spread of syndicalist and similar
theories among the more radical union leaders. The miners, the
railwaymen, and others began to look to nationalization for a
solution of their troubles. During the war, state direction and
control were shown to be practical propositions. In 1918 the
Labour Party was transformed from a loose federation of unions
and Socialist societies into a national political organization which
included among its objects a Socialist aim. Afterwards amplified,
it read at the time of the 1959 General Election: 'to secure for the
workers by hand or by brain the full fruits of their industry, and
the most equitable distribution thereof that may be possible,
upon the basis of the common ownership of the means of production, distribution, and exchange and the best obtainable
system of popular administration and control of each industry
or service'. This was vague enough to appease the syndicalists
in 1918 without committing the party to any particular form of
common ownership.

After the 1959 election, Mr Gaitskell, the Labour Party leader,
suggested revising the constitution and particularly this clause,

and an intense controversy took place throughout the movement. Eventually the national executive decided that the old statement should be reaffirmed but 'amplified and clarified' by a new statement recognizing that both public and private enterprise have a place in the economy. There was mounting opposition, in which trade unionists were prominent, to any change in the constitution, and eventually the new declaration was included in the annual report to the conference in the autumn of 1960, when it was approved, but no change was made in the constitution itself.

Socialists became active in the trade union movement towards the end of the last century, and they were the focus of lively struggles at the congresses of the 1890s. In 1894, Keir Hardie moved an amendment to a resolution calling for the nationalization of the land, mines, minerals, and royalty rents which added the words 'and the whole of the means of production, distribution, and exchange'. This was carried, but in the ensuing years the Socialists lost ground, and the T.U.C. has not since advocated public ownership so sweepingly. The present wording in their constitution says they will endeavour to establish 'the public ownership and control of natural resources and of services; nationalization of land, mines, and minerals; nationalization of railways; the extension of state and municipal enterprise for the provision of social necessities and services; proper provision for adequate participation of the workers in the control and management of public services and industries'.

Many unions also include Socialist aims in their rules, some with a syndicalist flavour. They were adopted at various periods and do not necessarily represent the thinking of the unions today.

The T.U.C. attitude in 1944 was described in the statement on post-war reconstruction in which they said that their programme was intended as a part of a gradual transition of the economic system from unregulated private enterprise to public ownership and public control, but that certain industries, notably transport, fuel and power, and iron and steel, were of such importance to the life and well-being of the community that their immediate transfer to public ownership was essential.

After the Labour Government of 1945–50 had carried through the nationalization of basic industries and services – coal, gas, electricity, transport, and steel – the T.U.C. were cautious in their advocacy of further public ownership. They were indeed opposed to the denationalization of steel and road transport, and demanded their renationalization, but beyond that they showed no enthusiasm for the various commitments adopted, and then dropped, by the Labour Party from time to time for public ownership of such industries as cement, sugar, industrial assurance, flour milling, chemicals, heavy electrical goods, slaughterhouses, machine tools, and mining machinery.

In 1951, the General Council issued a statement on the public control of industry which was not precise in its conclusions but suggested that for the time being efforts should be concentrated on improving the structure and operation of industries already nationalized. It dwelt on the difficulties of extending public ownership to whole industries not already dealt with, and laid much emphasis on alternative forms of control, such as competitive ownership of firms or sections in industry, development councils, and, particularly, boards of control, with representatives of employers, workers, and independent members, which would have considerable powers of supervision over the industries to which they were appointed.

The report was adopted but a good many trade unionists were not satisfied and the following year the Congress passed a resolution instructing the General Council to formulate proposals for the extension of social ownership to other industries and services and for the democratization of those already nationalized.

The following year the General Council produced an interim report which limited new commitments to the nationalization of water supply. They promised, however, to discuss with the unions concerned the factors involved in a number of engineering industries, agriculture, and agricultural distribution. The adoption of this report, against a strong minority vote, was a major victory for those who believed in basing the method of control of any industry on its special needs over those who believed in nationalization for its own sake.

The promised discussions with the engineering unions were

delayed. The Confederation of Shipbuilding and Engineering Unions had produced their *Plan for Engineering* which proposed public ownership and other forms of control for various sections of the industry, but when Mr Arthur Deakin described this at a Labour Party conference as 'just a mumbo-jumbo of meaningless words and phrases' and 'the worst abortion ever conceived in the mind of man' the Confederation refused to meet the T.U.C. on it.

However, they eventually got over their pique. The General Council held intermittent talks with the engineering unions and the building unions, and by the summer of 1959 they had decided that the major part of the machine tools industry should be brought under public ownership and that there is a strong case for the extension of public ownership in the aircraft industry. They were in favour of public intervention in the building industry, including a National Building Corporation, and were considering the future of mining machinery. The 1958 Congress carried without opposition a resolution declaring 'the urgent necessity for the nationalization of Britain's basic industries, with priority for the key sections of the engineering industry'.

Earlier the T.U.C. had been slower to commit itself to new schemes of public ownership than had the Labour Party, but during the years that the General Council was by slow stages reaching its empiric conclusions about machine tools and aircraft, with a good deal of pushing from behind by congress delegates, the Labour Party was backing away from further nationalization. When told of the T.U.C.'s views, the party executive had to point out that the policy statement, *Industry and Society*, published in 1957, committed the next Labour Government to hold official inquiries before decisions on further nationalization were taken. Thus at the time of the controversy which followed the 1959 General Election, the T.U.C. was committed further in the direction of public ownership than was the Labour Party.

In spite of the traces of syndicalist thinking in some of the trade union rules, it can be said that syndicalism disappeared as an important force in the movement in the period following the 1926 General Strike, at least for the time being. Equally the 1952 Congress was said to mark the end of trade union belief in public ownership on principle. There has also, as was described in the last chapter, been a movement away from workers' participation in control.

What seems to have taken place is an instinctive recoil from ideals which, as they grew nearer to achievement, brought closer a threat to deprive the unions of their traditional functions and even of their reason for existence.

In the last chapter, it was pointed out that the unions seem to have given up the attempt to solve the problem of wages policy under full employment. The reason is simply that the problem can be solved only if restriction is imposed on the unions' primary function of trying to get improved wages and conditions for their own members.

The trade union movement has refused to accept the dilemma, and consequently offers no solution to it. They are in favour of economic planning and controls, but refuse to accept the planning or control of wages, which are one of the most important factors in the economy.

Public ownership presents the issue even more clearly than public control. It was shown in the last chapter how competitive collective bargaining brought the trade union movement into conflict with the Government over the wages of London busmen. The same thing has happened with the railways. It is bound to happen whenever a Government feels it necessary to restrain wage increases, and so long as every union is trying to do better for its members than every other union. The unions in nationalized industries can only win by threatening to damage the national economy. If the Government is determined, they cannot win, but the country may suffer.

So long as there is a mixed economy, there is a way out of the difficulty by fixing wages for workers in nationalized industries, like those in the Civil Service, by comparing them with those in private industry. But if all the major industries were publicly owned that would be impossible. No union would accept worse treatment from the Government than any other. The broad movement of wages would have to be decided by agreement between the Government and the unions as a whole, and national strikes on wage issues would be intolerable because every such strike would in effect be a general strike. Socialism, if it meant general public ownership, would mean the end of unions as we know them. It is not surprising that the unions have turned away from it. What is surprising is that they never discuss these problems.

Workers' participation in control raises another issue. If union representatives are part of management, are they to negotiate with themselves? That issue has been thoroughly discussed. Indeed it was the main reason that unions turned their backs on trade union representation on the boards of nationalized industries in the thirties. But the same issue arises, in lesser degree, whenever workers or unions are associated with management, whether in development councils, national advisory bodies, or joint production councils. It is dodged at present by creating an artificial division between wages and conditions on the one hand, and other sides of industrial life on the other, and by laying it down that joint advisory bodies must ignore the former. But a share in management which ignores one of the most important concerns of management must be inadequate.

So long as the individual unions are determined to preserve their prerogative to bargain on the wages of their members they must in practice reject Socialism and syndicalism and any participation in management that means much. Yet they mostly call themselves Socialists and are nearly all affiliated to a party which calls itself Socialist and still includes among its objectives the common ownership of the means of production, distribution, and exchange. And when the leader of the party asked them to change that, the trade unions objected more than anybody.

How they would deal with these issues if the Labour Party were again returned to office no one knows, least of all the trade unions. Certainly they have made no plans for it.

The association of the trade unions with the Labour Party raises a good many problems regarding the relationship of the T.U.C. with the Government, whether Labour or Conservative.

The T.U.C. itself is not affiliated to the Labour Party. Their representatives meet, on increasingly rare occasions, with each other and with the leaders of the Cooperative Union on the

National Council of Labour, but the Council has long ceased to play an important part in the movement. Two T.U.C. representatives may attend the meetings of the Labour Party home policy committee and two representatives of the Labour Party may attend meetings of the T.U.C. economic committee. They sometimes set up joint committees to consider special issues, for instance railway finances and coal mining problems. And of course there is a good deal of informal contact.

But while the party and the T.U.C. are independent of each other, both are subject to the control of the big unions. All the largest unions in the T.U.C. are also affiliated to the Labour Party. They have five-sixths of the vote at the party's Annual Conference. These votes are decisive in policy decisions and also enable them to control the election of a majority of the party executive. They have also about 100 M.P.s in the Parliamentary Labour Party.

The trade unions provide a substantial proportion of the party's finance. In 1958 the party's income from affiliation fees, at 9d. a member, amounted to £245,714, of which the unions contributed £209,549. Donations to a General Election fund amounted to £105,630, of which the unions provided £105,157. Unions also spent considerable sums in financing their own candidates.

This does not give the whole picture because the constituency parties are financed mainly by the subscriptions of individual members. They pay 6d. a month while the political levies paid by trade unionists average just over 2d. a month. Some unions, including at least one big one, the National Union of Teachers, have political funds but are not affiliated to the Labour Party. But since the number of union members paying the levy is more than six times the number of party members, it appears that the ratio of contributions is a little more than two to one.

Trade unionists do not have to pay the political levy. About one and three quarter millions of them are in unions which have no political funds. In unions which have a political fund, they may contract out of paying it by signing a form. This was the original arrangement laid down in the 1913 Trade Union Act. After the 1926 General Strike, the procedure was reversed so that members had to contract in by signing a form if they wanted to pay the political levy. The original position was restored in 1946, with striking results. In 1945 less than half the membership of unions with political funds paid the levy. In 1958, eighty-eight per cent paid it (922,000 had contracted out). The total paid rose from £224,000 in 1945 to £748,000 in 1958, during which time the average contribution rose from just under 1s. a year to just over 2s.

The difference to the Labour Party would appear to be well over a quarter of a million a year. The system of contracting out has been much criticized, particularly by Conservatives. It is argued that members may hesitate to take the necessary step for fear of bringing themselves into disfavour with their workmates, though there has been little evidence of undue pressure. On the common assumption that three million trade unionists do not vote Labour, it seems probable that a good many contribute to the funds of a party which they do not support. Twopence a month may not seem worth bothering about.

The question is really whether the force of inertia should be on the side of the Labour Party funds or against them. Since the political activities of the union are the result of a majority decision by ballot vote, it is not unreasonable to expect members to fall in line with the majority decision unless they specifically ask to be excused. After all, unions affiliate to the Labour Party primarily because they believe they will benefit their members by doing so.

It is sometimes asked whether a Labour Government can be expected to act in the interests of the people as a whole, when the party from which it is formed is thus subject to the domination of one vested interest. But in practice the Labour Government after the war did on a number of occasions act in a way the unions opposed.

On a long term view, of course, the unions did control the Government's policy. They had the controlling voice at the annual conferences which made the party's various policy decisions. They had power to control the executive which drew up policy documents and on them based their election manifesto. But the Government could and did decide the timing and the practicability of implementing these decisions in the light of the circumstances of the day.

The more critical the public becomes of the unions, the more reluctant they are to entrust power to a party over which the unions exercise so much control. Labour's defeat in 1959 was attributed in some measure to this attitude.

Mr Frank Beswick, one of the Labour Party's defeated M.P.s, put it shortly after the election in these words: 'If we are to replace profit-seeking capitalism, then we must be able to show how trade unions are to fit into the new scheme of things. So far their leaders have shown little indication that they are prepared to accept any other role than the protector of their members' rights – in a public no less than a private concern. It may well be argued that this remains the first duty of a trade union. But in that case there are several millions of voters who will not accept that this pressure group should occupy a predominant place in the control centre of a political party which hopes to form an alternative government.'

Before 1959, the trade unions were always regarded as the main strength of the Labour Party, as indeed for the most part they remain, but after that year's election some voices on the political side were heard talking about the possibility of separating the two sections of the movement.

At the same time there seems to be a tendency for trade unionists to turn away not so much from the Labour Party as from political action. The *News Chronicle* trade union Gallup Poll in 1959, shortly before the general election, suggested that seventy-one per cent of trade union members intended to vote Labour, a higher proportion than for some years, while only seventeen per cent intended to vote Conservative.

But more than half of them, fifty-five per cent, thought trade unions should not be concerned with political matters like the H-bomb and foreign affairs. In recent years the T.U.C. have somewhat weakened their association with the Labour Party. They have been reluctant to commit themselves to party policy statements in detail. As has already been remarked, the National Council of Labour has been allowed to lapse into unimportance.

The link with the Labour Party creates not only external difficulties, but internal ones which are growing more serious as the manpower of industry changes in character. Probably the main reason why the National and Local Government Officers' Association and the National Union of Teachers and some other unions have remained outside the T.U.C. is the dislike of many of their members for its political associations. Those who support affiliation make much of the 'independent' position of the T.U.C., but their opponents are not convinced. There are many other unions who accept the independent status of the T.U.C. and affiliate to it for the industrial advantages which they believe affiliation gives them, but have no political funds and are not affiliated to the Labour Party. The number of unions affiliated to the Labour Party at the end of 1959 was eighty-seven while the number affiliated to the T.U.C. was 184 (the figures are not exactly comparable) but the affiliated membership of the party was more than two-thirds that of the T.U.C.

Many non-political unions, like N.A.L.G.O. and the N.U.T., are associations of white-collar workers. Among those in the T.U.C. which are non-political are the Civil Service unions, with the single exception of the Union of Post Office Workers, the bank employees, some insurance unions, those of actors, variety artistes, journalists, scientific workers, professional footballers, and the London County Council staff.

Whenever the T.U.C. takes some obviously political step, such unions are anxious about the effect on their members and still more anxious about the effect it will have on recruitment. Usually they quietly abstain from voting on political resolutions, but at the 1957 Congress they made a formal declaration of their intention to abstain on an economic resolution which urged all trade unionists to campaign for an early return of a Labour Government.

The bank employees and others of these unions were much disturbed when the 1959 Congress invited Mr Gaitskell to give an address as a prelude to the Labour Party's election campaign, but were somewhat relieved when Mr Gaitskell made what amounted to a declaration of mutual independence, assuring his listeners that neither the Labour Party nor the unions would ever attempt to dictate to the other.

Though some non-manual unions are active in the Labour

Party, the reluctance of many white-collar workers to join the T.U.C. because of its association with the party is a serious disadvantage. They have also been alienated, more than manual workers probably, by the unofficial strikes and other activities which have brought unions into public disfavour.

The problem is likely to grow more important because the proportion of white-collar workers is steadily increasing in Britain, as in other countries. In the United States, they exceeded in numbers the blue-collar workers (their name for manual workers) for the first time in 1956.

In Great Britain the proportion of non-manual workers in the main manufacturing industries rose from 16 to 21·2 per cent in the ten years between 1948 and 1958. In addition to that there is the long-term, continuing shift in the labour force from agriculture and fishing, and to a lesser extent from manufacturing, mining, and building, to the service industries such as transport, distribution, finance and insurance, the professions, sport, and entertainment, which employ a much higher proportion of non-manual labour.

The growth of public ownership and public services is one factor which has led to the strengthening of white-collar unions. The larger the employer, the easier organization becomes. Not only trade unions proper but professional bodies like the British Medical Association and even an employers' organization like the National Farmers' Union have negotiated regularly with the Government on behalf of their members, and in doing so assumed some of the characteristics of a trade union.

Some of the non-manual workers' organizations, for instance those of the teachers, local government officers, and bank employees, have been among the most rapidly growing unions in the post-war period. White-collar trade unionists probably number some two million now – more than a fifth of the total – yet there is no question that they still represent the widest field for future recruitment, and a growing one. But they have not got the political traditions of the manual workers. Unless their attitude changes, recruitment will continue to be hampered by the political associations of the unions.

All the strains in the relationship between the party and the unions were intensified by the long and bitter controversy over nuclear disarmament which began in June 1959, when the annual conference of the National Union of General and Municipal Workers, always previously the most faithful supporters of the establishment, startlingly passed a resolution in favour of unilateral nuclear disarmament by Britain. The device of calling a special conference of the union in August, at which the decision was reversed, made certain the adoption of the official policy on defence at the T.U.C. Congress at the cost of much cynical jeering at the union's stratagem.

Meanwhile at his biennial conference in July that year, Mr Frank Cousins had issued his challenge to the official policy and secured the backing of a large majority of his delegates. After a pause for the General Election, the battle was resumed at every trade union conference in 1960. The leaderships of all the big unions, except the Transport and General Workers', were in support of the official policy but three of them, the Union of Shop, Distributive and Allied Workers, the Amalgamated Engineering Union, and the National Union of Railwaymen, were defeated by their delegates, in the last case by one vote.

At the 1960 Congress the official policy was again saved by a manoeuvre, this time on the part of the leaders of the A.E.U., who ignored the fact that the official policy and the T.G.W.U. resolution were mutually contradictory and voted for both. Once again the day had been saved, or half saved, at the cost of making the trade unions an object of ridicule. But at the Labour Party conference a month later no trick could be found to save the official policy. Unilateralism triumphed.

There followed Mr Gaitskell's declaration of war against the decision and a battle throughout the movement.

All sorts of conclusions were drawn from all this. There were renewed attacks on the union block vote (which will be discussed in a later chapter). Some people on both sides began to wonder whether the alliance should be preserved. On the one hand it was argued that the unions had placed the politicians in an impossible position. On the other it was suggested that the unions should not allow themselves to be embroiled in the political issues which divided the party but should concentrate on industrial issues. The feelings of those who disliked the political activities of the unions certainly became stronger.

On the whole, however, it was accepted that there was a genuine difference of opinion in both sides of the movement on a fundamental issue, and that the inevitable struggle (apart from the doubtful stratagems employed by some unions) did not reflect any basic fault in the relations between unions and the party.

In spite of their link with the Labour Party, the T.U.C. were able to maintain reasonably friendly relations with the Conservative Government from 1951 to 1955. They were helped in this by the fact that none of the General Council are members of the Labour Party executive, to which most unions send their second strings, and only one or two are Members of Parliament, so that they are not individually involved in decisions made by the Tories' political opponents.

Nevertheless there have been some awkward situations, particularly just after the Conservatives had been returned. The T.U.C. at once made their famous declaration that it was their long-standing practice to work amicably with whatever Government was in power and the Government soon showed their readiness to continue the practice of consulting the T.U.C. on all matters affecting the workers.

But it was not always so easy. The Government might well hesitate about taking the union leaders into their confidence on matters on which they would shortly be debating with the T.U.C.'s allies in the House of Commons. The Labour Party, on their side, were anxious lest the T.U.C. should commit the movement on important issues, before they reached Parliament, without the party being consulted.

There was a lot of argument among the union leaders, for instance, when the Government invited the T.U.C. to discuss the proposed Bill to denationalize steel. Some said they should not help to draw up a measure to which they and their political allies were opposed, while others said they should take every opportunity to ensure that the Bill took account of the interests of the workers in the industry. They decided in the end not to enter into discussion until the Bill was actually drafted. The problem has never come to a head since then.

It may be true that the trade unions could have more influence with a Conservative Government if they were not allied to the Labour Party. In the United States and many other countries, the unions have no constitutional political alliance and act as a pressure group whatever party is in office, as they did in this country in the last century. There does not appear to be much public feeling about it, however. Criticism of the alliance comes mainly from Labour's political opponents.

THEY JUST GROWED

Brother Fights Brother – Bridlington Bonds – Bag's I Do It –
Drilling Holes and Chalking Marks – Trying to Sort them Out

THE structure of the British trade union movement is quite irrational. It has grown up that way and the will to straighten it out has never been strong enough to be effective.

In most industries there are many over-lapping unions, organized on different principles. To begin with there are the craft unions, many of which laid enduring foundations about a hundred years ago. They aim to include all the members of a particular skilled craft, sometimes mainly in one industry, like the Typographical Association, but often in many industries, where-ever such craftsmen are found, like the Amalgamated Engineering Union. Then there are the general unions, which grew up from 1889 onwards, organizing labourers and unskilled workers and anyone else not already organized. About the same period there began to appear occupational unions, organizing people in one non-craft occupation, such as clerical and other non-manual workers. In the period before the First World War the theory of industrial unionism spread rapidly, and unions like the National Union of Railwaymen were formed, usually by amalgamation, which aimed at organizing everybody in a single industry, from labourers to craftsmen and white-collar workers.

The general unions, who organize anybody, overlap each other in almost every industry. Craft unions have boundaries which increasingly overlap as industrial techniques change. The would-be industrial unions are an obvious threat to the craft, general, and occupational unions operating in their industries. Some unions have a local or limited character and become rivals to broader based unions catering for similar types of workers.

To add to the confusion, some old craft unions, such as the engineers, gradually widened their scope to include semi-skilled and unskilled workers and even women, and thus overlapped the other unions in their industry, becoming in a sense an industrial union for their own industry, while also organizing craftsmen in all other industries. Occasionally disgruntled sections of a union break away from it, after which there is always bitter antagonism.

The three big strikes in 1955 resulted partly from inter-union troubles, and in the succeeding years there was a succession of local demarcation disputes, the causes of which seemed so absurd as to arouse ridicule. Members of the public were given the impression that the unions were motivated only by narrow self-interest, were completely lacking in a sense of proportion, and were incapable of managing their own affairs in a reasonable way.

There are three main causes of friction – wage rivalry, poaching, and demarcation. Rivalry over wages and conditions is often connected with competition for membership. Obviously, the union which appears successful in improving wages and conditions is likely to attract members. It may, however, be simply a matter of prestige and status. Often the issue is the differential between the pay of craftsmen and others.

The 1955 strikes illustrate several of the different kinds of conflict. The strike which closed the national newspapers was called by the maintenance craft unions, the Amalgamated Engineering Union and the Electrical Trades Union, because they resented the priority given to the printing unions in negotiations from which they were excluded, though their members' wages depended on them indirectly. They held that they were forced merely to follow behind the others, without the right of genuine negotiation.

There was a somewhat similar dispute in the steel industry the following year, arising from a demand by ten craft unions for an improvement in the relation of their wages to those of the process workers organized in the Iron and Steel Trades Confederation which, despite its name, is more of an industrial union than anything else.

The railway strike of 1955 arose out of the conviction of the Associated Society of Locomotive Engineers and Firemen that footplate staff had been unfairly treated in a wage settlement with the National Union of Railwaymen. The railways provide the classic example of conflict between an industrial union and others. It has been going on since the N.U.R. was formed by amalgamation before the First World War with the express purpose of creating an industrial union. The A.S.L.E.F. and the Transport Salaried Staffs' Association, which organizes white-collar railway staff, have maintained their independence, but they watch every action of the N.U.R. with suspicion. The N.U.R. has some engine driver members and there is constant bitter rivalry. The three unions cannot agree on a common wage policy, and more than once in recent years have each put forward different pay claims. The T.U.C. has tried to induce them to work together but the industry remains the only one of importance in which the unions have still no kind of coordinating body or federation. Railway passengers have probably not suffered for the last time because of this strife.

The dock strike of 1955 belonged essentially to the group of poaching or jurisdictional disputes. In 1954, the National Amalgamated Stevedores and Dockers, a small union previously confined to London, recruited members of the Transport and General Workers' Union in Hull, Birkenhead, Liverpool, and Manchester. They then claimed negotiating rights in those ports, but the T.G.W.U. successfully resisted their claim. The employers, who said it was for the unions to decide who represented them on the various joint negotiating committees, were helpless. Other issues raised by this dispute will be discussed elsewhere in this volume. Here we are only concerned with it as one of the rare examples of a poaching dispute resulting in a strike. Such disputes are frequent but are usually settled peacefully by direct negotiation between the unions or through the disputes machinery of the T.U.C.

They arise when one union recruits members or former members of another union, or begins recruiting at some plant where another union claims prior rights. If either asks for it, the T.U.C. will set up a disputes committee to adjudicate between the unions. The awards are almost invariably honoured.

The awards are made according to principles laid down in the

'Bridlington Agreement' adopted by the 1939 Congress, revising the 1924 'Main Principles for the Avoidance of Disputes'. In general the agreement is based on 'squatter's rights' – that is to say that once a union has established itself among any particular group of workers, no other should interfere. The agreement recommends that unions should make working agreements with each other regarding spheres of influence, mutual recognition of membership cards, machinery for composing difficulties, and conditions for transfer of members. A union should not accept a member of another union without inquiry or where inquiry shows that the member is under discipline, engaged in a trade dispute, or in arrears with contributions, and should not start organizing activities where another union has the majority of the workers employed or negotiates wages and conditions, except by arrangement with that union.

If the committee is satisfied that members have been poached, there has usually been a recommendation that the offending union should 'return' such members or 'cease to take contributions from them'. In an average year the T.U.C. has seven or eight such cases to consider. Between the end of the war and 1958 there were ninety-six.

In 1958–9 there were nine cases, including the last episode in the long story of the dispute between the stevedores' union and the T.G.W.U., and the chalk lines dispute at Cammell Laird's, referred to later. The blast furnace men and the Iron and Steel Trades Confederation asked for a ruling, in advance, as to which should organize at a new lime-burning plant. The A.E.U. complained of organizing activities by the National Union of General and Municipal Workers at three different works. The T.G.W.U. and the Association of Supervisory Staffs, Executives, and Technicians asked for a ruling about employees of the Glasgow Corporation Transport Department recruited by A.S.S.E.T. The T.G.W.U. and the National Society of Metal Mechanics asked for advice regarding the application of the Bridlington Agreement to the request of two workers to transfer from the former to the latter. There was a dispute between the T.G.W.U. and the Amalgamated Society of Woodworkers as to who should organize the workers at a firm manufacturing plug doors and hatches.

It will be noticed that in several cases the unions were asking for rulings before they had reached the stage of dispute.

In addition to the general Bridlington Agreement, there are numerous bilateral agreements between unions regarding such matters as spheres of interest and recognition of cards. The Transport and General Workers' Union and the National Union of General and Municipal Workers also have a standing joint committee to deal with difficulties as they arise.

It is sometimes argued that overlapping and competition between unions are to be encouraged because they keep the unions on their toes and prevent the growth of bureaucratic tendencies.

Jurisdictional disputes and the methods of settling them raise questions about the rights of the individual which will be discussed later. Demarcation disputes raise no such issues, but the trade union emotions which give rise to them go deeper. For that reason they are generally more intractable. While jurisdictional agreements on spheres of influence help rather than hinder industry, demarcation rules can be and often are a constant brake on efficiency.

They are concerned with what groups of workers should do a particular job, and are no doubt as old as craftsmanship. They may be based on broad principles – only a painter may use a brush, only a joiner may use a screwdriver and so on. Or they may be based on custom in a particular place, sometimes the result of an ancient struggle. It is to the interests of the employer that there should be a clear understanding, so that friction and delays may be avoided, and demarcation agreements are often set out in writing. In the north of England, for instance, there is to be found a building industry demarcation list several pages long.

The unions argue that such rules help to maintain quality and avoid danger of injury by ensuring that work is done only by men qualified to do it. The main object of them, however, is to preserve opportunities of employment for the craft concerned. These rules have been screwed up and tightened during periods of unemployment until they have become in some cases incredibly rigid. Everybody has heard absurd stories of such rigidities, some of them no doubt exaggerated, but the bare truth can be hard to believe.

An example that has often been quoted from the shipyards is the fitting of a portlight, which requires a shipwright to mark the position of the light, a caulker to make the opening, a driller to make the sideholes, and a caulker to bolt the light and attach the chain. Each tradesman has to be summoned by his foreman and the operation carried out in sequence.

Similarly, in house building, a painter, whose main job may have been finished days before, has to be recalled to wash down and finish off, even if it means a long journey for half an hour's work.

These rules obviously slow down work, and their cost to industry is far greater than that of the occasional actual strike. The latter may be either between unions and employers or between different unions.

Disputes with employers often arise when skilled jobs are broken down or changed until they are no longer skilled, but are still claimed by craftsmen, with craft pay and conditions. The result is usually a compromise, which makes the work unnecessarily expensive. One result is that employers are slower to introduce new methods than they would otherwise be.

An example of this kind of difficulty arose in the construction of concrete houses where the concrete is poured into standardized moulds. The employers said no skill was required and the work should be done by labourers. The woodworkers claimed it, however. Eventually it was agreed that the work should be done by 'balanced gangs', consisting of one or two carpenters and seven or eight labourers.

The most familiar type of dispute occurs when more than one union claims the right to do the work. At one time in 1955 work had been delayed for several months on six building sites in different parts of the country, including two power stations, a factory, and a school, because of disputes about who should fix the metal windows. The joiners, who fix windows of traditional types, naturally claimed the work almost everywhere. Their claim was challenged, at one place or another, by half a dozen other crafts. Perhaps the plumbers were the main contestants, but there were also the heating and ventilating engineers, the bricklayers, and, where the windows were fixed in stone, the masons. They were even in one case claimed by the brass and metal mechanics. The position was complicated by the fact that the manufacturers of metal windows sometimes trained their own men to fix them.

A new type of patent wall panel, delivered with a finished surface, was claimed by plasterers, bricklayers, and joiners, while the employer claimed that it should be handled by labourers.

Comparatively recently both the woodworkers and the plasterers claimed the work on patent suspended ceilings of fibre tiles. An agreement was reached based on whether any plastering was done or not. Then it came to light that some roofing contractors were putting slaters and tilers on the job and trouble broke out again.

Then there is the ancient feud between the plumbers and the heating fitters as to who should lay certain pipes – which still causes occasional stoppages. The heating fitters say the plumbers should stick to cold water pipes as anything to do with hot water is their prerogative. The plumbers insist they can handle any kind of pipes. The material of which the pipes are made is also a factor.

Most difficulties arise out of new developments. The increasing use of factory-made units in building sets continual problems for unions – and employers. They will have to find a more radical solution of their problems sooner or later.

While delays from such disputes are not unusual, stoppages of work are rare. The National Federation of Building Trade Operatives has a committee to deal with them and puts pressure on unions to reach a settlement; and usually they do so, though there may be delay and the eventual solution may not be the most economical one.

In shipbuilding there have been notorious strikes, such as the 'drilling holes' and 'chalk line' disputes at Cammell Laird's yard at Birkenhead, but even in shipyards the strikes are few. The demarcation problem in shipbuilding is said to have begun when the shipwrights, being workers in wood, decided not to enter the metal trades when iron ships began to appear. Other craftsmen became responsible for making the metal parts of the ship. In recent times the work of the platers and shipwrights has often overlapped. Coppersmiths, engineers, and plumbers have quarelled over the work on pipes. Shipwrights and joiners have both claimed certain woodworking operations.

As a classic example of its kind, I propose to print in some detail the description of the hole-drilling dispute at Cammell Laird's given by the court of inquiry under Professor D. T. Jack which reported in March 1956.

In September 1953, the company received an order to build three insulated fruit-carrying vessels. The keel of the first vessel, *Calamares*, was laid on 4 October 1954, and she was launched on 2 September 1955. By June 1955 the time was drawing near for taking in hand the insulation work for the refrigerated cargo holds. The company looked upon this part of the construction as a large and, in detail, unfamiliar job, as regards both design and method. The insulation coverage and air-ducting were to be in aluminium.

That there were seeds of trouble in allocating or 'demarcating' this work amongst the various trades concerned the company knew from past experience. When, therefore, in June 1955, the joiners (Amalgamated Society of Woodworkers) claimed all the work in connexion with insulation, the company had it in mind that it was the established practice in their yard for certain work on aluminium to be done by the sheet metal workers (National Union of Sheet Metal Workers and Braziers).

They suggested to the joiners and sheet metal workers a joint, informal meeting in the hope that a friendly agreement could be achieved. They regarded this meeting, however informal, as fulfilling the procedure of the General Demarcation Agreement, 1912, between the employers federations and various unions, which, precluding any stoppage of work, lays down the steps to be taken to deal with such a dispute.

At the meeting, on 25 August, the joiners claimed all the insulation work, whether metal was involved or not, but to arrive at an amicable settlement were prepared to 'concede' the preparing and cutting of the metal to the sheet metal workers. The sheet metal workers replied that all metal work was theirs. The company took the view that the custom and practice was for sheet metal workers to carry out all the operations on aluminium, including cutting in the shop and fitting in place on board ship. Where it was fixed to wood the joiners secured it and where it was fixed to metal the sheet metal workers secured it.

The meeting adjourned and for the next meeting, on 1 September, the company put forward a draft agreement which would have given the sheet metal workers the cutting to size of all aluminium sheets and sections, the joiners the drilling and securing of all aluminium sheets and sections to wood, and the two trades half each of the work of drilling and securing of all aluminium sheets and sections to metal.

This was the first mention of drilling. The drillers (a section of the Ship-constructors' and Shipwrights' Association) had not been brought into the discussion. On consideration, the employers got the word deleted from their draft.

The sheet metal workers persisted in claiming all the metal work and two more meetings were fruitless. The company sought to invoke the formal procedure of the 1912 agreement, but the joiners, according to the other two parties, refused. The joiners said this was because the metal workers wanted to introduce extraneous matters. Claiming that the company was allocating the work to the sheet metal workers, the joiners struck on 12 September, after a partial stoppage on 8 September.

Following a number of meetings with a conciliation officer of the Ministry of Labour, two understandings were signed on 21 October 1955. The first, between the company and both unions, gave the measuring, marking, and cutting to size of aluminium sheets and sections to the sheet metal workers, and the securing of aluminium sheets and sections to wood, after fitting by sheet metal workers, to the joiners, the securing of metal to metal being left over for later settlement.

The second understanding between the company and the joiners, which became the crux of the situation, said: 'It was agreed between the parties that the operation of drilling aluminium sheets and sections attached to wood after fitting by the sheet metal workers shall be joiners' work.'

Thereupon the drillers, who had still not been brought into the negotiations, threatened to strike if joiners attempted to drill metal on board ship. The joiners claimed that the drilling under-standing had given them the right to drill all the holes required for the aluminium sheets to the exclusion of the sheet metal workers. The sheet metal workers, supported by the company, claimed that in the preparatory work in the shops they should drill or punch about four-fifths of the screw holes, the rest being drilled on board as necessary. They did not claim to drill holes on board ship and the drillers did not claim the drilling of holes done in the shops.

The company now decided that the drilling understanding was unworkable and informed the joiners that it could not be carried out. The joiners, who had returned to work after the October understandings, went on strike again and were still out in March, in spite of repeated efforts by the Ministry of Labour and later by the T.U.C. to bring about a solution.

The inquiry laid most of the blame on the joiners, and recom-mended that the dispute should be dealt with under the 1912 agreement. The men returned to work after the issue of the report and a month or so later a joint committee, set up under the 1912 agreement, awarded the work to the drillers. Some 500 workers had been on strike and a rather larger number laid off over a period of seven months, and the building of a big ship had been seriously delayed.

During the hearings by the committee of inquiry the company said they did not mind who did the work so long as it was done efficiently and economically. It is a remarkable fact, however, that the committee's report contains no reference at any other point to such questions as which trade was best qualified to do the work or how the work could be most efficiently organized.

After this long struggle it might have been supposed that steps would be taken to prevent a repetition of the stupidity, but nothing was done. In the hole-boring dispute, the T.U.C. General Council was brought in on an appeal by a union whose members were affected, though they were not directly involved. About a year later, the General Council themselves took the initiative in intervening in a dispute between the same two unions at the Glasgow shipyard of Alexander Stephen and Sons, the other shipyard which has been most affected by strikes, and succeeded in bringing about a resumption of work.

In the autumn of 1958, yet another stoppage occurred, this time arising from a dispute as to whether drillers or welders should operate a stud-welding gun. The issue had been in dispute for many years. When on one job the firm divided the work between the welders and the drillers, the drillers went on strike and shipwrights in the same union refused to work on docking ships.

Then in April 1959 came the chalk mark strike at Cammell Laird's, arising from a dispute as to who should make chalk marks on plates to show where cutting was to be done. Two members of the boilermakers' union, a welder and a burner, were instructed by their steward not to work alongside members of the shipwrights' union who, they considered, were doing their work. The firm refused to give the two men other work while the dispute was being discussed. Within a fortnight 1750 boilermakers were on strike and 2000 other workers had been laid off. The stoppage resulted in a loss of more than 200,000 working days.

Such strikes as these, perhaps more than any others, irritate the public because on the surface the causes seem so trivial as to be absurd. To stop a great shipyard because workers cannot agree as to who should make chalk marks has an air of the ludicrous. The heat engendered adds to the impression. An official of one union, whose members had been laid off, said they were 'innocent victims of the bulldozing and dictatorial tactics of another union', and that kind of abuse and counter-abuse is normal during such disputes. It is little wonder that the unions became a music-hall joke.

The issues are not trivial to the men concerned, however. The right to do a certain job means employment. That is important to all the unions in an industry like shipbuilding which is at the mercy of frequent fluctuations in demand. It is particularly important to those whose traditional crafts are being superseded by changed methods of production.

Demarcation disputes in printing are also frequent, usually resulting from the introduction of new methods. They often seem to have held up improvements in efficiency resulting from technical developments, but have rarely resulted in strikes. This is in large measure due to a firm rule of the Printing and Kindred Trades Federation that if unions cannot reach agreement about a dispute over demarcation of work or organization, no aggressive action or stoppage of work shall take place. The dispute must be reported to the federation, which must arrange within a fortnight for an arbitration board, the award of which will be binding.

The printing unions are among the most strongly organized and independent in any industry. Their rules lay down precisely who shall do what work, and this often results in waste of manpower and the use of skilled workers for unskilled work. The stoppage in the general printing and provincial newspaper offices in 1959 was partly due to insistence by the employers that there should be relaxations of some of the demarcation and other restrictive practices.

They asked, for instance, that Typographical Association craftsmen should be interchangeable instead of divided into three water-tight sections, and that apprentices should be trained in each of the sections; that there should be no demarcation of work within certain departments; that non-craft workers might be employed as type storemen and on proof pulling and other jobs; that non-craft workers might be employed in foundries and used on all processes apart from plate production; that in small foundries where a full-time stereotyper was not required, T.A. or other labour might be used for the work; that once manning arrangements had been established, the crew working under the craftsman in charge should cooperate in the various operations instead of each being restricted to a particular operation; and that when a firm changes from one process to another, existing labour might be retrained on the new processes.

The list gives some idea of the kind of difficulties that had been met by printing employers but in most cases, in so far as complaints about them are justified, the troubles are rather of the nature of restrictive practices than of inter-union disputes. Some of them were dealt with in the final settlement.

There was one inter-union dispute which almost stopped the national newspapers in 1953, but basically it was a jurisdictional rather than a true craft issue. When Associated Newspapers bought the *Daily Sketch* from Kemsley Newspapers they decided to print it at the *News of the World* office instead of Kemsley House. The *Sketch* had previously been printed with members of the Printing Machine Managers' Trade Society as machine minders, but at the *News of the World* office members of the National Society of Operative Printers and Assistants were employed as machine minders. Both claimed the work, though the operative printers offered to take existing *Sketch* machine minders into membership if they were transferred.

Two old trade union principles were in conflict – 'the custom of the house' and 'follow the job'. The issue was as to which was the overriding principle.

While the argument was going on, there was the Gilbertian situation, as a court of inquiry described it, that full teams from both unions were employed in the machine room, taking charge on alternate nights. The management paid the wages of both.

A stoppage of either the *Daily Sketch* or the *News of the World*, as nearly happened, would have stopped *all* the national newspapers because the Newspaper Proprietors Association have an agreement that if one paper is stopped, they all stop.

The trade union movement has long been well aware of the disadvantages of the overlapping structure. A good deal is done, as has been pointed out, to deal with its consequences. The printing unions' arrangements for arbitration on demarcation disputes have been mentioned. There is the 1912 agreement with the employers to settle such disputes in shipbuilding. The boilermakers' society is not a signatory but it has an agreement with the shipwrights, revised in 1959, which provides for immediate arbitration if local agreement cannot be reached. These agreements should have prevented the Cammell Laird and Alexander Stephen and Sons strikes. The National Federation of Building Trades Operatives has in recent years appointed a committee to deal with demarcation disputes between member unions. It usually gets half a dozen cases a year. If a building dispute comes to the point of a strike it can be dealt with through the disputes machinery.

The T.U.C. has on occasion intervened to try to prevent or

settle strikes arising from conflicts between unions nationally, for instance, in the 1955 railway and newspaper strikes and again in the 1960 railway dispute, and locally it has intervened in one or two of the shipbuilding demarcation disputes, but rarely until after a stoppage has continued for some time. The procedure for dealing with jurisdictional disputes, as has been remarked, usually works effectively.

Periodic efforts have also been made to improve the structure of the movement. From 1874 to 1924 nine resolutions were passed by the Trades Union Congress on trade union organization. The 1924 resolution said that the number of unions should be reduced to a minimum and instructed the General Council to draw up a scheme for organization by industry and a scheme to secure unity of action, without actual merging of unions, by linking them scientifically to present a united front.

After three years of inquiry, the General Council reported that it was impossible for a body such as the T.U.C., composed of all types of unions, to reach agreement on any specific form of organization. The most they could achieve would be to remove the main causes of friction in the day-to-day working of the unions, and to facilitate negotiations for amalgamations and for various forms of closer unity. They recommended the amalgamation of unions with closely related trade interests and, pending amalgamation, that they should make joint working arrangements with a view to joint negotiation on rates of pay and working conditions, and the elimination of competition for members and of overlapping.

In 1943, Congress returned to the subject, asking the General Council to prepare a report on uneconomic overlapping and competition, what amalgamations were desirable, and structural and other changes necessary to ensure maximum trade union efficiency in the future. In their report the following year the General Council said: 'It is clear that the liability of inter-union competition has still to be faced. . . . The general council are of the opinion that this overlapping and competition are detrimental to the prestige and efficient working of the trade union movement. It is confusing and irritating and the reason for it is beyond the comprehension of many members and most non-unionists. It is uneconomic if only because of the time, energy, and money devoted by unions either to keeping up their end in the struggle or, alternatively, in the settlement of disputes (both inter-union and industrial) which arise.

'There is still the trade union organizer who, instead of extolling the advantages offered by his own union, will attack the rival union. This type of propaganda, particularly among non-unionists, may result in an attitude of "a plague on both your houses".'

However, the General Council again came to the conclusion that any basic alteration of trade union structure was impracticable. They said that schemes of amalgamation, federation, and joint working should be developed wherever possible. 'In a changing world, the trade union movement cannot retain its pre-war conception of organization if it is to be fully efficient.'

Where amalgamation was not yet possible, they advocated the development of federations which would be closely linked with the T.U.C. These federations would be largely responsible for economic functions of unions, that is to say collective bargaining and the formulation of industrial policy. Such federations would embody the principle of industrial unionism and could efficiently conduct and coordinate the work, provided their affiliated unions were prepared to afford them the necessary facilities and staff.

On the other hand, administrative functions, in which they included collection of contributions, payment of benefits, educational work, and general servicing of members, would remain the responsibility of the individual unions.

The third group of functions centred on recruitment as the focal point of inter-union competition. After considerable argument, the report concluded that the federations should guide the main work of trade union recruitment. Once spheres of influence had been determined, either geographically, on the basis of the job, or on the basis of the firm, it would be clear to which union a new entrant would belong. 'The saving of time, energy, and money involved in a catch-as-catch-can method of organization would enable a much higher standard of trade union service to be rendered by all unions concerned and result in a higher and more stable membership within each union.'

The report advocated that the T.U.C. system of advisory committees should be developed to cover each industry, service, or related group; that the federal body concerned should be associated with each advisory committee; and that T.U.C. research facilities should cover all industries and be available to federations.

It was a well thought-out scheme but produced little result. The General Council held a long series of meetings with groups of unions, most of them fruitless, but detailed proposals, industry by industry, were worked out in later reports. There have been one or two important amalgamations since then. The unions in the miners' federation united in the National Union of Mineworkers about that time. The two big organizations of distributive workers came together to form the Union of Shop, Distributive, and Allied Workers. There was a substantial amalgamation of hospital unions and others in the furniture and foundry industries. Apart from the absorption of a few small unions by larger ones, little else has been achieved.

In 1958 the General Council made a survey of what had been achieved since 1946, but had nothing more to say except to urge improvements in schemes of joint working. The following year they had discussions with the three big federations in engineering and shipbuilding, building, and printing, but found they had no desire for closer links with the T.U.C., and that the individual unions had no desire to give up their autonomy.

Yet the unions have been well aware that technical progress, by destroying old divisions between crafts and classes of workers, has made their out-of-date structure an increasing liability, and repeated efforts have been made to carry through amalgamations. The bringing together of craft unions where demarcation has become artificial is indeed a more urgent matter than the absorption of small unions or the merging of larger unions catering for the same class of workers.

The Amalgamated Engineering Union brought twenty unions to an amalgamation conference in 1956 and the United Society of Boilermakers brought seven shipbuilding unions together a few months later. Nothing came of either meeting.

The building unions have spent a great deal of time in recent years discussing the implications of technical developments for trade union organization, but have not done anything about it. Proposals for amalgamation of the plumbers and the heating fitters were defeated in the ballot of the latter. More determined negotiations have taken place in the printing industry, in one case between the two big general unions, the National Union of Printing, Bookbinding, and Paper Workers and the National Society of Operative Printers and Assistants, and the other at first between nine craft unions. Neither has yet succeeded. More recently proposals for amalgamation were discussed by the paper workers and the London Typographical Society. Negotiations between the British Actors' Equity Association and the Variety Artistes' Federation were successful, but in the ballot of members (which is a statutory obligation), the V.A.F. turned the plan down. The same thing happened to negotiations between the National Union of Journalists and the Institute of Journalists.

With the best will in the world, it requires great patience and determination to carry through a merger. The 1927 and 1944 reports both listed the five main obstacles in this order: fear of loss of trade identity and autonomy; marked differences in scales of contributions and benefits; disinclination to pool resources with a union in a weak financial position; conflicting policies on bases of organization, wage policy, and general affairs; and difficulty in placing officials.

The more unions there are taking part in negotiations, the greater the difficulty. A vigorous small union is often more reluctant than one that has lost its vitality to merge its identity with a larger one.

While progress with amalgamation has been slight, progress towards more powerful and better equipped federations has been negligible. The Confederation of Shipbuilding and Engineering Unions was greatly strengthened by the reaffiliation of the Amalgamated Engineering Union, but otherwise the hoped for federal development did not take place. While now, as in 1944, several federations and many joint bodies unite in negotiations on wages and conditions, the number of T.U.C. advisory committees has not been extended and consultation between the federations and the T.U.C. has become little if any closer. There are no new federations and none of them, with the exception of the National Federation of Building Trade Operatives in a minor way, has any responsibility for recruiting.

Indeed, one of the most astonishing things about the trade union movement is its failure to plan or carry out major recruiting campaigns among the millions of unorganized workers. The T.U.C. annual report in 1958, when affiliated membership was a little more than 8,300,000, suggested that, by the time it reached its centenary in 1968, it might have reached 10,000,000. Since membership had increased by only half a million in the previous ten years that seemed improbable, and it actually fell in 1958–9. Even if it were achieved, more than half the employees in the United Kingdom, numbering some 22,000,000, would remain outside the movement.

The T.U.C. organization committee in 1955 analysed the affiliated membership to see in what sections it was weakest. They decided that a national recruiting campaign was impracticable from the point of view of staff and finance, and that in any case the unions would rather do things their own way. Trades councils were urged to undertake more recruiting campaigns but little came of it. An attempted national campaign to recruit women evoked little response.

Only about a quarter of the women employees and a little over half the men are union members. Nor are the non-unionists by any means confined to occupations in which organization presents special difficulties, such as agriculture, distribution, catering, domestic service, and certain professional services. It has been estimated that, in the engineering industries, organization is little over fifty per cent and in building, textiles, chemicals, clothing, pottery, and a number of other manufacturing industries it is considerably less. Large numbers of workers are recruited every year, particularly by the general unions, but large numbers also drop out.

Unsatisfactory as it is in many respects, the structure of the British trade union movement has great advantages over those of many other countries. First among these advantages is the fact that the T.U.C. is the only national centre. In America the movement was long split by a division over craft and industrial organization, and the miners and others still remain outside the main centre. In many European countries they are split denominationally by Catholic and Protestant unions or politically by Liberal and Communist unions operating side by side with a main, largely Social Democratic federation. In some countries there is a separate centre for white-collar workers.

In Britain, the T.U.C. represents 8,100,000 out of 9,600,000 trade unionists, and there are only two big unaffiliated unions, the National and Local Government Officers' Association and the National Union of Teachers. Over the years, too, the number of unions has been growing fewer while the membership has increased.

At the end of 1958 there were still 304 unions, out of a total of 657, with fewer than 500 members, but they included only 0.5 per cent of the membership of all unions. At the other end of the scale almost half the total membership was in seven unions with more than 250,000 members each and eighty per cent was in thirty-six unions with more than 50,000 members each.

Nevertheless development is not fast enough to keep pace with the changing shape of industry. Many leaders see that changes are required but have not the determination to carry them through. Many will not surrender their kingdoms for the general advantage.

The weaknesses in trade union structure at branch and plant level will be conveniently discussed in the next chapter.

5

ROBBER BARONS

TRADE union organization is a source of power. Full employment and other factors have increased that power in recent years, especially in the workplace. There it may get into wrong hands and be irresponsibly used. There have been examples in recent years of local trade union chiefs establishing themselves in a position in which they can dictate to the employers and defy the authority of their own union – and even that of the law. 'Little Napoleons' they have been called by Mr Victor Feather, T.U.C. assistant general secretary. Such men are commonly the leaders of unofficial or wildcat strikes, the frequency of which has so disturbed public opinion.

These little Napoleons may have a recognized position in the union as branch officials or shop stewards, or they may be the unofficial leaders thrown up by unofficial strikes. The most barefaced boast of power to defy the law came from a fully accredited officer of the Transport and General Workers' Union who has repeatedly gone his own way – Mr Spencer Tribe, the union market organizer.

It happened like this. In 1954 a butcher demanded that his purchases at Smithfield Market should be handed to his employee rather than loaded by one of the licensed market porters, who are members of the union. The market tenant, fearing a strike, refused to allow him to take the meat. The butcher brought an action in the Mayor's and City of London Court to establish his right to carry away his purchases. He secured a judgement in his favour and damages against the market tenant. The men nevertheless threatened to strike if he took the meat away and were successful in preventing him from acting on the judgement. 'He said he would, the judge said he could, we said he could not and he did not,' commented Mr Tribe.

During the war and in the ensuing period the market branches of the union, at Covent Garden as well as at Smithfield, established a dominating position because they had tight closed shops, which enabled them to control the labour supply, and because they were dealing with many small employers whose interests conflicted and who were vulnerable because they dealt in perishable goods. A sudden strike imposed losses which could not be recovered, but usually the implied threat of a strike was sufficient.

More will be said of the markets when we come to deal with restrictive practices. It may be remarked in passing, however, that the vulnerability of an employer in special circumstances has contributed to some of the most distasteful unofficial strikes of recent years. For instance, there have been a number, particularly by electricians, to get additional payments in the last few weeks before exhibition buildings are completed. With the usual rush to get everything ready in time, and great pressure from exhibitors and others to avoid delay, the temptation to get a little extra out of it has been more than some workers could resist.

Local dictatorships by union branches, such as those at the markets, are comparatively rare, except perhaps in the coal industry. Much more often they are established by shop stewards. The irresponsible power which they sometimes exercise arises partly from the failure of the unions to adjust their local structure to modern conditions.

Shop stewards have emerged comparatively recently in many industries as an important element in union organization. Representing the union in the factory or other place of work, they have a responsible and thankless job, for which they receive negligible payment, and the great majority are worthy and painstaking servants of the membership.

The T.U.C. has estimated that there are altogether at least 200,000 shop stewards or their equivalents. The Transport and General Workers' Union have probably more than 25,000 and the Amalgamated Engineering Union about 22,500. Most unions now provide for them in their rule books but their functions are seldom clearly defined. Usually they are responsible for union recruitment, for seeing that dues are paid regularly, for ensuring that industrial legislation and agreements are observed, and for the representation of members' interests to the management.

In a statement on productivity in 1948, the T.U.C. General Council referred to the need for developing the functions of shop stewards, and making available the best qualified workers in the shops for these responsible duties. 'Too often', they said, 'it is the practice to allow the shop steward to be appointed and then to leave him pretty much to his own devices. One unfortunate result of this is that some shop stewards, taking a wrong view of their duties, are tempted to misuse their powers. Some of them heve been drawn into unofficial organizations whose claims to leadership of the shop stewards cause them to transgress the authority of the unions to which they belong and to take an independent line of action, often to the detriment of the union interests and the well-being of the workers whom they claim to represent. It frequently happens that the worker best suited to serve as shop steward is, partly for these reasons, unwilling to undertake the duties.

'The General Council urge upon union executives that the training of shop stewards in the elements of production and costing, industrial relations, representation of the workers, and relations with management is a question to which the unions must now address themselves with energy and determination.'

Since then the T.U.C. itself and some unions have provided opportunities for this kind of training, but not with sufficient energy and determination to ensure that the majority of shop stewards receive it.

The danger of the system, as at present operated, lies in the lack of clearly defined responsibility, either upwards or downwards, particularly in a plant where there are many different unions. Union administration is based on the branch. Where there is only one union concerned, and where the branch is based on the place of work, the shop steward will take his instructions from branch officials and report back to it.

In most unions, however, the branch covers all the members living in a geographical area. It can exercise little control over shop stewards in a firm in which it may have only a few members. Moreover there may be twenty or more unions with members at a single plant. They all have their shop stewards who commonly set up a shop stewards' committee with a convenor or chairman, an office of considerable power in a big factory but usually unrecognized in either union rule books or agreements with employers.

In industries for which the Confederation of Shipbuilding and Engineering Unions negotiates, officials of joint shop stewards' committees have to be endorsed by the confederation and are responsible to its district committee, but it is not easy for district officials to keep in touch with all the firms in their area. There is no organization of members to which a joint shop stewards' committee has to report. They may call a mass meeting if they wish, but this is outside official union organization. Shop stewards are the only link between most members and their union, and their voice is commonly regarded as the voice of the union.

Obviously they are subject to few organizational restraints. Sometimes they build a well-financed little empire for themselves, and so long as the workers follow them, they can defy the union leadership.

The most remarkable illustration of this was at Briggs (now Ford) Motor Bodies at Dagenham. The machine, and the way it worked, was described in some detail in the report of a court of inquiry into a dispute there (the 'bellringer' dispute) in 1957. The company, which had been taken over by Ford's a few years earlier, employed about 9,000 workers at the Main and River plants. Twenty-two unions were recognized, of which the Amalgamated Engineering Union was the most important. The company negotiated directly with the unions' leaders.

There was an agreement on procedure for the settlement of disputes which said: 'The parties agree that, at each stage of the procedure set out in the agreement, every attempt will be made to resolve issues raised and that until such procedure has been carried through there shall be no stoppage of work or other unconstitutional action.'

There were 160 shop stewards at the two plants. Each was elected by the members of his own shop, and, as in most shops there were a number of unions, he represented members of other unions as well as his own. There was a shop stewards' committee for each plant and a joint shop stewards' committee for the two combined. This body elected members to a joint works committee representing employers and employed, so that it had a certain official standing.

The joint shop stewards' committee financed themselves by the sale of lottery tickets, from which they received an income of £16,150 in five months. Some £9,339 went in prizes, £2,066 to the expenses of shop stewards on union business, £1,900 on various forms of strike activity, and £400 to a central fund, the purpose of which never appeared. They had £3,118 in the bank. The committee maintained their own well-equipped office and joined with similar committees at other Ford works to publish a twopenny monthly periodical with a sale of 10,000.

The A.E.U. district committee, which had the responsibility of ratifying Briggs A.E.U. shop stewards, consisted of seventeen members, of which six were from Briggs and three from Ford's works.

In the period after the signing of the procedural agreement, from August 1955 to March 1957, there were 234 stoppages of work, often without discussion or warning of any sort and almost impossible to trace to any particular source. Often the first the company heard of trouble was that men had stopped work and gone home. Many of the stoppages were, of course, small and local.

Eight of the thirteen trade union members of the joint works committee were said to be Communist Party members.

The court, while also making criticisms of the employers, concluded that a section of the shop stewards' organization at Briggs was largely identified with the unfortunate state of affairs existing there. Influential members of the shop stewards' organization, their report said, had used their powers to encourage resort to unconstitutional methods in the conduct of differences and disputes, contrary both to the terms of the procedure agreement by which they were bound and also to the advice and exhortations of their national union officers.

Communists had made use of the shop stewards' desire to protect their own interests and powers to the further detriment of good industrial relations, with consequent damage to production, but this had not been the prime cause of the trouble. The continued existence of such an uncontrolled organization was against the interests of the unions, the company, and the work-people alike, and was a potential obstacle to the creation or continuance of harmonious labour relations.

A shop steward empire also existed at London Airport. Civil aviation is another highly vulnerable industry, because the loss resulting from a stoppage is very high and cannot be recovered. Actual strikes have been rare because the tendency has been to give way to unofficial pressure until it is felt to be intolerable.

In British European Airways the breaking point came with the 'Peters case', as it was called, in January 1954, when the corporation took action to control shop stewards' activities and effected some improvement. The British Overseas Airways Corporation did not rebel until four years later, when a stoppage arising from a ban on overtime was followed by a court of inquiry.

It was reported to the court that unconstitutional action of various kinds – mass meetings during working hours, bans on overtime, strike threats – had occurred among B.O.A.C. engineering staff thirty-six times from 1953 to 1958. There had been forty-four such incidents among all B.E.A. staff in the same period.

The employers contended that the existence of the joint shop stewards' committee cut across the constitution of the national joint council and its sectional and local panels – the complicated official joint machinery. The shop stewards machinery at London Airport differed from that at Briggs in that individual shop stewards are elected by and represent only their own union members. (Seventeen unions are represented on the national joint council.) It was clear there, as at Briggs, that some national union officials were encouraging the unofficial elements.

A remarkable feature of this inquiry was the evidence given by Mr Jim Matthews, of the National Union of General and Municipal Workers, then the secretary of the employees' side of the National Joint Council, but not accepted by other national union officials. He identified the trouble-making element as the Communist Party cell which he said had been set up at London

Airport and encouraged by the weakness of the two corporations. He asserted that leave had been give to Mr S. Maitland, chairman of the B.O.A.C. joint shop stewards' committee, who, he said, was secretary of the London Airport branch of the Communist Party, to take part in the strike at J. Lyons and Company in 1954.

He quoted examples of Communist activity at London Airport and referred to the part played by Mr Maitland on previous occasions, alleging that, in the 1958 strike, Mr Maitland had received encouragement from certain trade union members of the national joint council. He asserted that the constitution of the joint shop stewards' committee cut right across accepted procedure, and that 'unscrupulous individuals' among the shop stewards were misleading and confusing their workmates. These individuals, he said, had carried out to the letter at London Airport instructions for shop stewards issued by the Communist Party in 1955.

The court accepted the view that the dominant figure in the joint shop stewards' committee was Mr Maitland, who was a Communist. They were satisfied that the Communist Party did not hesitate to act in a disruptive manner and that Mr Maitland's activities were of that kind. They accepted that Communist Party membership at London Airport was very small but added: 'The danger is that organizations such as shop stewards' committees, if left to their own devices, may fall under the influence of a few men of perseverance who are prepared to exploit the loyalty of their fellow workpeople for their own ends. . . . The curbing of disruptive elements presents a problem for the trade unions but it is also a problem for the rank and file. . . . The trade unions have entered into solemn agreements on behalf of their members but these members do great disservice to themselves and their unions if they give their support to individuals who are prepared to sabotage those agreements.'

The court also thought that the militant elements had been encouraged by inadequate leadership and that shop stewards and their committees should have their powers more clearly defined and circumscribed.

The years 1959 and 1960 were notable for a constant succession of unofficial strikes called by shop stewards in the factories of the British Motor Corporation and other firms in the motor industry. The shop stewards' committees at the various B.M.C. factories had formed a joint shop stewards' committee which they endeavoured to extend to other firms in the motor industry. The driving force seemed to be at Austin's where the shop stewards, under Communist leadership, had their own publication and an elaborate organization, though there was relatively little trouble at Austin's. The Communists were less important in some of the other B.M.C. factories with a bad record.

The number of workers taking part in most of the strikes was small, but the industry is so closely knit that thousands of others in numerous plants were often laid off in a very short time. The unions accused the firm of doing this unnecessarily to try to make the strikers unpopular.

In January 1959, a strike of some 200 Birmingham crane drivers and slingers threw some 6000 others out of work. The following month a strike of 300 door assemblers made 9300 others idle. In the first months of 1960 a walk-out by 300 press shop men at Ford's affected 5000 others, a walk-out by 132 fork-lift drivers and maintenance men in the Rootes group affected 8000 others, an official strike of fifty-two maintenance electricians in a B.M.C. factory affected more than 30,000 others, and a strike of fifty-one internal transport drivers at a B.M.C. factory affected 22,000 others. Perhaps the most notable strike from this point of view, affecting motors indirectly, was that of 1700 British Oxygen workers in October 1959, which made 60,000 workers idle. Most were in the motor industry, but other industries affected included general engineering, steel, railway workshops, shipbuilding, and electronics.

The past history of the motor industry helps to explain why the shop stewards have been able to get such a hold in some firms. During the past twenty years thousands of new recruits have come into the industry from many parts of the country and from many different occupations, first for war work and then to meet the post-war world's demand for cars.

The managements engaged in hectic competition for workers in which expense was no object. Every kind of financial and other inducement was offered to attract workers, with a reckless disregard for the future. Earnings soared until in Coventry, and scarcely less in Birmingham and London, they became a by-word. Little attempt was made to create or maintain a balance of wages between one factory and another or even between different groups of workers in the same factory.

Almost any demand from the shop stewards was met. Since local earnings far exceeded the national rates negotiated by the unions, the workers naturally tended to look to the shop stewards for leadership. Many of the newcomers to the industry, without any sense of loyalty to it, found things so good that they did not bother to join their unions, and some of the employers seemed to think that all the labour policy they needed was to hand out lavish wages and lavish benefits.

The birds came home to roost with a vengeance as soon as the first beginnings of a recession hit the industry. The shop stewards found they could no longer get their own way as a matter of course. Tougher resistance from the employers resulted in longer: strikes. Some of them were over the dismissal of shop stewards one at Austin's in 1951, another long and bitter one at the same firm in 1953, officially backed by the National Union of Vehicle Builders, over the refusal of the firm to re-engage a shop steward who had been made redundant. In 1957 there was the dispute at Briggs over the dismissal of a shop steward which led to the court of inquiry referred to above. In 1959 there was another major dispute over the dismissal of a shop steward at Morris Motors. Some of the employers became no less aggressive than the men.

The number of working days lost through disputes in the vehicle building industry, mainly in motor manufacture, rose from 60,000 in 1949, to 132,000 in 1950, to 266,000 in 1951, to 468,000 in 1952, and to 589,000 in 1953. And these figures exclude workers in other factories made idle as a result of a dispute elsewhere.

The 1953 figure was not exceeded until 1959, but little strikes grew more and more frequent as the struggle for power between the managements and shop stewards spread from firm to firm. The unions built up their membership to 100 per cent in some firms and began to strike against the employment of non-unionists.

Only Vauxhall's and until 1959 Rootes, both of which in their different ways had devoted a lot of attention to labour relations, were able to keep clear of the battle. The number of strikes in the vehicle building industry rose from 46 in 1949 to 176 in 1960, in which year 586,000 working days were lost.

The large number of unions involved in the motor industry, as at London Airport, made it very difficult for the official leadership to handle the situation. No fewer than twenty-one are represented on Ford's national negotiating committee and not many fewer have members in most of the other firms. All the unions are in the Confederation of Shipbuilding and Engineering Unions, but the confederation is concerned with many other industries, as is the engineering employers' federation to which the firms, except for Ford and Vauxhall, belong. There are no separate bodies for the motor industry alone, and the national engineering agreements pay no special regard to the factors peculiar to motor manufacturing.

Ford's have had their own problem in the integration of Briggs Motor Bodies, where there had been a long history of trouble before they took it over. B.M.C. have had an even greater problem to coordinate the policy of the merged Austin and Nuffield organizations, with quite different wage systems and conditions.

That unofficial strikes can and do occur without the prompting of lower-level union officers, such as shop stewards and branch committees, is evidenced in the docks.

'It appears to me incredibly easy to bring dock workers out on strike,' remarked the report of the 'Leggett Committee' which inquired into unofficial stoppages in the London docks in 1951. 'We were given repeated instances of men stopping work almost automatically, with little or no idea of why they were stopping. In the words of one witness, himself a dock worker, "all that was needed was for a man to go round the docks shouting 'All out!' and waving the men off the ships, and out they would come". Many dock workers, themselves firm supporters of constitutional methods and resolutely opposed to the activities of unofficial elements, told us frankly that it was too much to expect of the average dock worker that he should remain at work when his mates were out, irrespective of his opinion of the merits of the dispute. He was quite likely to join a strike without even inquiring about the reasons for it.'

There is no office on the docks comparable to that of shop steward. There are so many disputes about the handling of cargoes that offices manned by full-time union officials have been established within easy reach of every point on the docks. In 1951, the Transport and General Workers' Union, to which most dockers belong, had ninety full-time officials for a regular dock membership of 65,000.

Having no shop stewards to lead them in defiance of the official union leadership, the dockers create their own unofficial organization, which rapidly takes charge of a strike and almost always succeeds in holding the men's loyalty, despite all the union's efforts, until they decide the time has come to call it off. After the first big post-war strike in 1945, the unofficial leaders established the National Portworkers' Defence Committee, with a national chairman and organizer and five regional committees with representatives from ports that had not taken part in the strike. They said their aims were to take up victimization cases, to secure control of the union machinery and 'clean it up', and to continue in being until the unofficial machinery could be merged in the union itself.

This machinery seems to have continued in some form, with its own monthly publication, during most of the post-war period. The Leggett committee, which was set up after there had been four major strikes on the London docks in three years, regarded the starting-point of the Portworkers' Committee as the 'zinc oxide' strike of June 1948. Members of the unofficial group, they said, played an important part in the Canadian Seamen's dispute, and in the strike of April 1950, following the expulsion from the T.G.W.U. of three of its members.

'It is our belief', the Leggett report commented, 'that those who direct the activities of the unofficial group have no interest whatever in strengthening or reforming the organization of their respective unions (as they claimed). Indeed, many of them do not appear to have taken the trouble to inform themselves about the constitutional working of the unions. In our view they are more concerned to disrupt the working of the port as often and as seriously as possible than they are to improve dock workers conditions.'

Conceding that some members of the group might be sincere men who did not appreciate the destructive purpose behind its activities, the report went on to describe the group's technique in staging a strike:

'The first step is usually the summoning of a mass meeting "on the fields" just before either the morning or the midday call. The more level-headed men stay away from these meetings, and those who attend seldom represent anything like a majority of the workers in the area. After some inflammatory speeches, a resolution to stop work is carried, this process being helped on occasion by prolonging the meeting until it is too late for those present to attend the call, or until only a small number of supporters remain.

'Although only a small proportion of the workers concerned may have voted for the stoppage, this has usually been a sufficient nucleus to start the trouble. Indeed, false statements are often made that a stoppage has already commenced. Once a stoppage has reached substantial proportions, the tendency is for many of the men, particularly those living at a distance from their work, to stay at home and wait for news of a resumption from the Press or the wireless.

'The strike leaders continue active until a stage is reached where a movement towards resumption of work begins to appear. At this point the unofficial group has usually convened a mass meeting to gain for themselves the appearance of getting the men back to work, and to give as good a semblance as possible of retaining the men's allegiance. We have, however, been unable to trace any improvement in wages or working conditions as a result of strikes organized by this group. . . .

'The unofficial group have always worked to extend the area of stoppages, both within the Port of London and through contacts with other ports and even contacts abroad.'

The report referred to the 'sustained and systematic attack by unofficial spokesmen and publications on all union action, paying no regard to the merits of any particular issue, and characterized by unrestrained personal abuse of union leaders'. They added that certain leading members of the Portworkers' Committee were members of the Communist Party and that the political bias of the *Portworkers' News* was apparent.

Union officials are never more helpless than during dock strikes. During the 'zinc oxide' strike, the T.G.W.U. convened a mass meeting in the Albert Hall, so the unofficial strike committee countered by calling a mass meeting in Victoria Park at the same time. The Albert Hall meeting voted for a return to work and the Victoria Park meeting voted by a large majority for continuing on strike. The number of dockers on strike remained unchanged.

A Ministry of Labour report on the Manchester overtime strike in 1951 said that an organization seemed to have been created in Manchester all ready to take advantage of the dispute when it occurred. This organization obviously owed its origin to the Portworkers' Committee in London and the unofficial leaders seemed to gave gone to unusual lengths to keep the strike alive. The chairman of the Manchester Portworkers' Committee, Mr G. Norman, was an avowed Communist who played a dominant part in the strike. The court of inquiry into the overtime strike in the London docks in 1954 remarked that the committee still existed and that they had no reason to suppose that its character and activities or the character and activities of its adherents had undergone any appreciable change. Communists have usually played an important part in dock strikes; but they seldom seem to have initiated them.

Perhaps the most extraordinary of all dock strikes, however, was that in the summer of 1949 in support of the Communist-led Canadian Seamen's Union, engaged in a dispute in Canada which was partly a fight with the Canadian shipowners and partly an inter-union struggle.

Led mainly by Communists, London dockers involved themselves in the Canadian dispute to the extent of a strike lasting a month, in the latter part of which more than 15,000 men were idle. Servicemen, to the number eventually of nearly 13,000, were brought in to handle the ships. About 400,000 working days were lost.

The intricate and almost incredible story was reviewed by the Ministry of Labour later in the year. They found that the Canadian Seamen's Union had prepared to pursue their quarrel in British ports before their own strike in Canada began; that the campaign in this country was founded mainly upon the support of members of the Communist Party and their sympathizers; that attempts were made by C.S.U. strike leaders, three of whom came to England from Canada, to involve British union leaders and, where these failed, to discredit them by lies and misrepresentation; that their propaganda was unscrupulous; and that there were violent incidents alien to the conduct of industrial disputes in this country.

Up to 1954, most of the strikes had a strong anti-union flavour and were accompanied by violent abuse of Arthur Deakin, the Transport and General Workers' Union general secretary. While the 'poaching' dispute between the National Amalgamated Stevedores and Dockers and the T.G.W.U. was at its height, this dispute became the main cause of trouble, but there were several occasions when some T.G.W.U. members unofficially supported an official N.A.S.D. dispute.

Some people thought that Mr Frank Cousins, with a more left-wing policy than Mr Deakin, would have more influence with the dockers, but when a large part of the Port of London was brought to a standstill in 1958 (because of a stoppage at Smithfield which arose out of a strike of meat transport drivers) the dockers, as usual, ignored the advice of union officials and accepted that of the unofficial leaders.

The alliance between dockers, transport drivers, and market men is one that has cropped up previously and has at times been given a loose organizational link, thus bringing together members of local union committees and unofficial leaders.

The tally clerks in the Port of London are a section of the port transport workers who have frequently gone their own way, ignoring the union, and though few in numbers they can cause serious trouble by stopping work. About 1500 were on strike in September and October 1960, and for about a month almost paralysed the work of the port.

The London Chamber of Commerce investigated the effects of

the strike on port users. They found it impossible even to estimate the total costs, but figures supplied by thirty-two shipping companies, less than a quarter of the total, recorded losses amounting to £1,300,000. The Port of London authority lost £400,000 in port dues alone. Vessels diverted to Continental and other ports numbered 196 and 125 sailed without working or incompletely laden or discharged. The cost of the strike to one firm importing grain was £20,000, to a timber importer £12,000, and to a meat importer £12,000. One manufacturer reported £20,000 irrecoverable lost turnover, another £10,000, a third a whole year's business with a big customer. The report of the Chamber of Commerce said that in the long term the damage done to Britain's reputation in overseas markets was even more serious than the financial loss.

Another group of workers who have always insisted on going their own way are the London busmen. They originally made special conditions for their entry into the Transport and General Workers' Union and have always considered themselves a section apart. Throughout the thirties their 'rank-and-file movement' was battling with Ernest Bevin. Strikes are comparatively few but unofficial bans on overtime or threats of bans are not un-uncommon. Indeed the seasonal schedules are rarely changed without some kind of trouble.

Of the 56,000 busmen employed by London Transport, 22,780 took part in a one-day strike in January 1949, about overtime payments. A strike of 14,400 in 1950 was over the refusal of the executive to present a new wage claim and over the recruitment of additional women conductors. Some 16,000 were in a six-day strike in 1954 over revised schedules. In the same year there was a ban on overtime to hurry along a wage claim. In 1958 there was a one-day strike to protest against new schedules and in 1960 an overtime ban to hurry a wage claim. All these were unofficial. During the events which led to the official London bus strike of 1958 the men's delegates repeatedly rejected the advice of the union leaders, who allowed themselves to be overruled.

From July to September 1960, unofficial seamen's leaders conducted two strikes, one during negotiations for a new agreement and the second in protest against the terms of settlement. Bitterly critical of the union leadership, they set up a National Seamen's Reform Movement, centred in Liverpool, which remained in existence when the strike was over and was said to be threatening new trouble in 1961. The imprisonment of some leaders and strikers under the Merchant Shipping Act aroused much controversy. The strikers received financial support from the Canadian District of the Seamen's International Union of North America, who were accused of trying to secure bargaining rights and the control of jobs in ships trading to Canada and on the Great Lakes.

The history of the threatened railway strike of 1960 suggested that the London and Manchester district councils of the National Union of Railwaymen were on the way to throwing off central authority. The London district decided on a token strike of their 40,000 members in defiance of the national executive and chief officials and the Manchester district declared that they would call their own strike at a later stage if necessary. It was under the pressure of these threats that the national executive submitted a new wage claim, although an old one was on the way to arbitration, and then threatened to strike in breach of their agreements. For union leaders to surrender to local groups can produce worse effects than leaving them to act on their own.

Independent action by district committees is not unusual, particularly in organizations like the Amalgamated Engineering Union where officials are elected.

An unofficial shop stewards group in the electricity supply industry began to operate in the winter of 1959–60, apparently under Communist influence. They held meetings after each stage in the wage negotiations and in March 1960 they passed a resolution in favour of a three-day national stoppage in the power stations, 'working to rule' (which means going slow), and a ban on overtime. Mr Foulkes, the Communist chairman of the union side of the National Joint Council, had previously appeared to hint that such unofficial pressure would not be unwelcome.

Some unofficial strikes are spontaneous outbursts over genuine and, it may be, long-standing grievances. But most are part of a struggle for domination, going on all the time between management and men's leaders, with the national union officials intervening from time to time, usually to try to end the stoppage, since unofficial strikes infringe union rules as well as union–employer agreements. Such are the disputes at Ford's, the B.M.C., London Airport, the London markets, many coal mines, and some shipbuilding yards.

In unions whose whole-time officials come up for re-election every few years, efforts to bring a strike to an end may be half-hearted. The paid official has to remember that his job will soon depend on the votes of the men on strike and others like them. At the same time, he is aware that he does not depend on the national executive and general secretary for his position, and may well ignore them. Where a district committee or union headquarters are Communist dominated, little effort seems to be made to end strikes. Sometimes unofficial strikes are recognized. More often dispute benefit is paid after they are over, which makes it possible for the strikers who need it to get national assistance for their wives and families while the strike continues.

It does not follow from the last paragraph that strikes are more common in unions with elected officials than in those in which officials are appointed. In the latter – the Transport and General Workers' Union for instance – the officials feel their main responsibility is to the national executive and bureaucratic tendencies develop. Workers sometimes think that their interests are being neglected and are the more ready to take unofficial action which is directed at the union as much as at the employer. The balance of advantage in the two systems is hard to decide.

This is a convenient place to consider the impact of unofficial strikes as a whole. I have already referred in Chapter 4 to demarcation strikes, which are usually unofficial but may not be, and I shall be mentioning in Chapter 8 the numerous little stoppages which take place in shipbuilding and elsewhere, for instance to hold or finish a meeting, and which have the nature of a restrictive practice rather than a dispute.

Such little stoppages are usually most frequent, as at Briggs Motor Bodies, where the struggle for domination between the management and the men's workplace leaders is most intense. For the most part they do not appear in the statistics of the Ministry of Labour, which relate to stoppages of work due to disputes connected with terms of employment or conditions of labour and exclude stoppages involving fewer than ten workers, and those which last less than one day, except any in which the aggregate number of working days lost exceeds 100.

The Ministry's statistics do not distinguish between official and unofficial strikes. Indeed it would be very hard to do so, since some are recognized locally but not nationally and sometimes dispute pay is granted some while after the strike is over. Some strikes are declared official by some of the unions involved but not by others. Nor do the statistics give a complete picture of the effect of strikes, as those made idle indirectly as a result of a strike are only included if they are employed in the establishment affected. It is common for workers in other firms to be laid off. In most recent years, there has been a small number of big official strikes and a large number of unofficial ones, which, with a few exceptions such as those on the docks, are small. The best indication of the trend of official strikes is the number of working days lost and the best indication of the trend in unofficial strikes, the number of stoppages.

In 1959, for instance, 5,250,000 working days were lost, of which 3,500,000 were in the official printing dispute. On the other hand, there were 2073 strikes, of which only seven were in printing. Nearly half the recorded strikes in 1958 lasted not more then one day and another quarter not more than two days. Less than eight per cent lasted more than a week.

The strongest impression received by anybody analysing the figures for the first time is the almost microscopic amount of time lost in proportion to the total work of the country. In mid 1959 there were 22,347,000 employees, so that the loss of 5,250,000 working days represented less than a quarter of a working day per employee – perhaps two hours a man a year. If we exclude the printing strike, as it was official, then we are left with forty minutes a man a year. Some other strikes were official so that the actual figure is probably about half an hour a man a year. So about 0·02 of the nation's working time was lost through unofficial strikes. Some ninety-eight per cent of employees were not involved in any strike.

The three worst industries for unofficial strikes were mining, vehicle building, and shipbuilding. In mining, where there were 1292 stoppages, more than half the total for the country, more than four-fifths of the men were not involved in any strike (some were involved in more than one) and the average loss of time was less than four hours a man a year.

In vehicle building, nearly nine-tenths of the workers took part in no strike (again some took part in more than one) and time lost was rather more than half a day a man a year – say five hours. The figures would be rather worse for motor manufacturing alone.

In shipbuilding, nearly nine-tenths of the workers took part in no strike and the loss of time was about one and a third days a year – say twelve hours. But about two-thirds of the time lost in shipbuilding was in the chalk mark strike by boilermakers at Cammell Laird's, which was recognized by the union. If that strike is excluded, the average time lost was about four hours a man a year.

Though the impact of unofficial strikes is far less than that of absenteeism, accident, or illness, it is nevertheless true that their number has increased over the years and they probably cause more industrial dislocation than the actual figures suggest. In the most troubled period of British industrial history, from 1910 to 1913, the average number of strikes was just over 920. There were more than 1000 in 1918, 1919, and 1920 (1607), but after that there was a sharp decline. In the General Strike year, 1926, there were only 322. They did not exceed 1000 again until 1941, but in each of the years 1944–6 they exceeded 2000. Then they fell below 2000 until 1955 with a bottom figure of 1339 in 1950. The average for the years 1955–9 was more than 2500 – the largest number in our history. The number in 1959 had gone down to just over 2000, mainly because of a smaller number in coal mining, but in 1960 it was up again to 2797.

Experience since the First World War suggests that strikes are frequent only when employment is high, and consequently the workers can indulge in them with impunity. But it would be foolish to regard unofficial strikes as entirely the work of trouble-makers. Some employers fail to realize that different kinds of labour relations are necessary in full employment conditions. Managements which are provocative or pay insufficient attention to labour relations help the trouble-maker to establish himself. So do unions which fail to keep in touch with their members or neglect the interests of small sections of them. Tradition has a lot to do with it. You must go far back in history, for instance, to find the causes of the constant stoppages in the mines in some areas. The frequent major strikes in the docks were no doubt part of their restless adjustment to the unaccustomed disciplines of the dock labour scheme.

When all is said, it remains true that Britain seems to have more unofficial strikes than any other country. They are a serious problem in some firms in a few industries. The only coal-fields in which they are common are Yorkshire, Scotland, and South Wales. Some motor manufacturing firms, some shipyards, some ports are almost free of them. Many whole industries have practically none. In many others they occur at rare intervals. Whenever managements have devoted much attention to labour relations, over a long period of years, they are rare or unknown.

Unofficial strikes are indeed, with some exceptions, not so much damaging in themselves as symptoms of failures in management or union policy. They indicate the existence of bad labour relations, which must be having a serious effect on efficiency in other ways, and their effect is to make relations worse.

Unions seldom impose penalties on unofficial strikers, though it is almost invariably a breach of rule to strike without official authority. Practice in this respect varies, however. The Iron and Steel Trades Confederation, who attach much importance to the observance of agreements, invariably take disciplinary action, even sometimes expulsion. At the other extreme the National Union of Mineworkers never seem to take any action, though their rules are broken and their agreements dishonoured hundreds of times every year, and the Communist Electrical Trades Union adopt a policy of treating every strike as official unless they find reasons to decide otherwise.

Of the other big unions, neither the Amalgamated Engineering

Union nor the Union of Shop, Distributive, and Allied Workers takes disciplinary action. The National Union of Railwaymen and the Transport and General Workers' Union have done so rarely, and the National Union of General and Municipal Workers more frequently. After the British Oxygen strike of 1959, for instance, the N.U.G.M.W. suspended 112 members at Birtley, Co. Durham.

There is always a danger that such action will provoke a renewal of a strike. Three unofficial leaders were expelled by the T.G.W.U. for their part in the Canadian Seamen's strike in 1950, and 14,000 dockers struck for ten days in protest. Altogether seventy-seven members had to face union committees of inquiry to explain their activities in five major dock strikes between 1945 and 1954. Only the three mentioned were expelled. Others were cautioned or debarred from holding union office for a time.

'I don't think it would help to stop unofficial strikes if we expelled more people', Mr Arthur Deakin said once. 'It is much more likely it would increase unrest. Once men are expelled the union can have no more influence over them. It is much better that we should maintain our influence rather than weaken it by expulsions.'

Another consideration, where more than one union is operating, is the fear of driving members into the arms of a rival.

There are some industries, of which mining and the docks and building are conspicuous examples, in which, because of the changing and unpredictable nature of the work, disputes about a piece-work price or unpleasant and dangerous conditions may crop up unexpectedly and need to be settled on the spot. If such a dispute goes into the negotiating machinery the job will have been finished before there is a decision so that the men's chance of effective resistance will have gone. It is now or never if they are going to strike. In such industries there is especially need for immediate arbitration on the spot if agreement cannot be reached. As things are, unions are apt to be tolerant of unofficial action in such cases.

In some countries there are Labour Courts which can impose fines on men (or employers) who break an agreement. The system is said to work well in Sweden and Denmark. In this country there has been a somewhat similar arrangement for more than fifty years in the boot and shoe industry under which the union or the employers' organization can be fined if their members bring about a stoppage of work lasting more than three days. It has only on rare occasions been necessary to invoke this procedure.

In 1959 newspapers suddenly began to describe unofficial strikes as 'wildcat' strikes, a term that had been used in the United States for many years. It appeared to have the effect of putting the strikers psychologically on the defensive and of intensifying the already great public irritation. A good many people were arguing at that time that they should be made illegal.

Union leaders were disturbed by this threat of legal action. Some of them were also becoming indignant because many of their members were frequently being laid off as a result of strikes by members of other unions and their funds were suffering as a result.

The National Union of General and Municipal Workers at their annual conference in Scarborough passed a resolution calling on the T.U.C., the Confederation of Shipbuilding and Engineering Unions, and all other trade union federations and joint negotiating committees to examine the problem of strikes which made other workers idle and to consider what steps were necessary to ensure that all unions likely to be affected were fully consulted and that the appropriate procedures of negotiation were fully operated before direct action was taken. Moving the resolution, Sir Thomas Williamson said there was a minority 'whose stupidity and antiquated methods are becoming intolerable'.

At the Trades Union Congress in September, Sir Thomas announced that the general council intended to conduct an inquiry into unofficial strikes and the position of shop stewards.

'The actions that are complained about', he said, 'are unjustified breaches of agreement which under no circumstances can be condoned by the movement. The breaking of agreements is bad enough, but the consequences in most cases have been much more serious. In some cases whole processes and whole factories have been closed down, and hundreds and thousands of innocent trade unionists, who have had nothing at all to do with the dispute, have been thrown on to the streets without wages and often without unemployment benefit. Vital production has been lost, orders have been delayed, and it is this action more than anything else which is likely to undermine the economy on which we depend to maintain full employment.'

T.U.C. leaders had been condemning unofficial strikes in a general way for many years but had made no concerted attempt to do anything about them – or to condemn specific strikes – until the British Oxygen strike during the 1959 General Election. The General Council condemned that out of hand, but it was nevertheless widely believed that the strike, focusing public impatience at the frequency of unofficial strikes, contributed to the Labour Party's defeat.

The success of the Conservatives in the election may have made the threat of legislation seem more real to the union leaders. At any rate, the General Council set to work on their inquiry into unofficial strikes with unusual expedition.

The first result was an interim report to the 1960 Congress. The report quoted figures to show the small amount of time lost per man through strikes. It stated that eighty-five out of 137 unions which replied to a questionnaire, with 1,268,000 members, said they had not called or been involved in any stoppage of work during at least the previous four years.

A good deal of blame was put on misleading press comment, poor management, and one-sided procedural agreements for the settling of disputes. But the report went on, with some courage, to advocate disciplinary action against members taking part in strikes contrary to the general policy and specific advice of their union. Unions were advised to forbid their members to take part in national shop steward centres or conferences, the aim of which was 'to usurp the policy-making functions of unions or federations of unions', and to condemn and, in case of repetition of an offence, withdraw the credentials of shop stewards who acted in defiance of their executives.

There was also a suggestion that executives might increase their information services so that there would be a greater awareness among stewards of the policy they should be supporting. The important subject of communications within unions will be discussed in a later chapter. In the autumn of 1960 there were indications that some big unions were acting on the advice of the report. The A.E.U. and N.U.G.M.W. particularly took action to stop their members taking part in unofficial joint committees. The five unions in the electricity supply industry made arrangements to maintain closer regular contact with their members. Both the A.E.U. and the T.G.W.U. decided to organize special meetings of representatives to their members in the motor industry. The Ford unions set up a committee to examine the complaints of an excessive number of stoppages at Dagenham.

In addition a number of arrangements were made for joint discussions with employers on labour relations problems. The T.U.C., albeit without any sign of enthusiasm, agreed to meet the British Employers' Confederation. The Confederation of Shipbuilding and Engineering Unions agreed to meet the engineering employers to talk about the motor industry. On the shipbuilding side they also agreed to meet the employers, but that they had often done before without result.

It appeared that a beginning was being made.

6

THE RED MACHINE

IN an old rule book of the Communist Party you can find it laid down that in all working class organizations or branches, where there were two or more Communists, a party 'fraction' had to be organized, subordinate to the appropriate party committees: 'Nominations for all important positions in the organization are made by the fraction after consultation and agreement with the competent party committee. In the same way the party committee can transfer members from fraction to fraction as occasion demands a concentrated effort on any particular organization.

'Every question to be decided by the organization or branch in which the fraction is working should be discussed beforehand by the fraction meeting. On every question on which a decision is reached the fraction members must act unitedly and vote solidly in the meeting of the organization in question. Failure to do this constitutes a serious breach of party discipline.'

You will not find that in their rule book today but the system of working remains unchanged. The reader may have noticed in the last chapter how often Communist influence was found to be strong where unofficial leaders secured a dominating position and strife was constant.

The Communists concentrate their attention on the workplaces. 'No matter how effective Communist work is outside the factory gates, it is work inside, by our factory comrades and organization, that is decisive,' Mr John Gollan, the party secretary has said. The sentiments are constantly reiterated. And wherever the Communists secure leading positions as shop stewards in the factories, there is trouble. They are prominent in B.M.C., in Briggs, at London Airport, at Rolls Royce in Scotland. They are strong among the miners in South Wales and Scotland and parts of Yorkshire, the three strike areas in the industry. They have their men on the docks.

'The power of one shop steward to wreak damage in his section of industry can be immense, especially if the local body to which he is responsible is Communist controlled or dominated,' Mr W. Carron, president of the Amalgamated Engineering Union, once said.

In recent years the Communists have considerably extended the coordination of shop steward activities. They have long had an organization called the Shop Stewards' National Council, which has its own publication, the *Metal Workers*. This organization prompts the calling of conferences of shop stewards in particular groups like B.M.C., or the motor industry as a whole, or the aircraft industry, or the shipyards. More recently Communists have been prominent in the National Committee of Shop Stewards and works committees which have been trying to promote unofficial industrial action in the electricity supply industry.

'The leaders of opportunism will resort to every trick to prevent Communists from getting into the trade unions,' wrote Lenin in 1920. 'It is therefore necessary to agree to any and every sacrifice and even, if need be, to resort to all sorts of stratagems, manoeuvres, and illegal methods, to evasions and subterfuges, in order to penetrate the trade unions and to remain in them, carrying on Communist activities inside them at all costs.'

The Communists are normally in favour of exorbitant wage demands and strikes, but they have opposed inter-union and demarcation disputes. They have been among the strongest supporters of industrial unions. They were against the poaching by the National Amalgamated Stevedores and Dockers, for instance. 'The existence of many demarcation questions can become a barrier to the workers in their struggle against capitalism,' wrote Mr Harry Pollitt in 1958. 'The problems that arise from them can only be successfully overcome if they are amicably settled between the workers on the job themselves, and every encouragement should be given for this to be done so that the full force of all the workers in a factory or industry is exerted against the common capitalist class enemy and never split or directed against particular sections of workers. The more effectively the workers are organized in unity in the factories, the more powerful can their shop stewards become.'

The general direction of party organization in the unions is undertaken by the industrial department at the Communist headquarters in King Street, London. There is an industrial committee on which many leading trade unionists serve, with advisory sub-committees for particular industries. Reports from factory groups (or fractions) go up to the industrial department through the machine, and instructions are sent down. It is a well-devised instrument for its purpose, and seems to work efficiently considering how few Communists there are to work it.

Working as a disciplined organization in this way naturally gives the Communists much greater influence in union affairs than they would otherwise have, though their methods tend to arouse antagonism. If all the Communists vote in the same way on a resolution, while the other union members are divided, they may have good hopes that it will be carried. In the same way, if they concentrate their support on one candidate for an office, while others divide their votes among several candidates, his chance of election is strengthened, even where the transferable vote system is used.

This effect is heightened by the apathy of a large proportion of union members. In some unions, less than ten per cent record their votes in elections for office. A fairly normal Communist vote of four per cent, which is useless for political purposes, may therefore be sufficient, in industry, sometimes to get their candidates in. The average attendance at branch meetings is probably of the order of five per cent. Something more will be said of this in Chapter 9.

It is not to be expected that a large proportion of workers would want to spend a lot of time on union business. Why should they? They have other leisure time interests. It is natural that the unrewarded routine work of branch administration, whether for its own sake or as the beginning of the road to a union career, should be attractive to comparatively few. That is why it is not usually hard to become a shop steward or branch official. If no one else will take on a job, there is usually a Communist who will. But the conduct of a man's union is important to him, and it might have been thought that more would feel it their duty to attend a branch meeting once a fortnight or once a month, and that more would take the trouble to record their votes in elections for office.

It is true that recording a vote, if it is to be useful, also involves finding out something about the candidates; but if a man goes to branch meetings at all regularly he is likely to know something of them. Most trade unionists have no idea what is going on in their unions. The majority of those who vote do not seem to be much influenced by the fact that a candidate is a Communist. The miners who choose Communist officials are not Communists, as parliamentary elections prove.

Another advantage which Communists have over others is that they are more unscrupulous in their methods. It is part of their doctrine that the end justifies the means. Once they have obtained domination of a union or section of a union they use every possible means to maintain their position.

One of the most repellent examples of this to be exposed to public notice was the 'Chapman case'. In 1957 Mr Tom Chapman was elected the Amalgamated Engineering Union organizer in north London, defeating a well-known and popular Communist by one vote. The division had previously been completely dominated by Communists.

Mr Chapman found that his work was deliberately obstructed by his colleagues and staff. Letters and notices did not reach him. He was given no information or wrong information about meetings. Unofficial strikes in the division became more frequent. He was inundated with petty demands and then criticized for not dealing with them promptly.

Mr Chapman appealed to the national executive, who conducted an official inquiry. 'There is no doubt whatsoever', said their report, 'that a concerted and sustained campaign has been carried out against Mr Chapman as divisional organizer.' There was some criticism of Mr Chapman's conduct of his duties but severe condemnation of the actions of a number of his colleagues. The assistant divisional organizer was suspended for a month without pay. The three full-time secretaries of district committees in the division were reprimanded. A woman employee who 'appeared to be determined to blacken Mr Chapman's character' was dismissed. A clerk in the north London office, a well-known Communist, was instructed not to attend district committee meetings, which he was not entitled to do.

Other surprising incidents, only less remarkable than those in north London, were reported from Sheffield, another A.E.U. district where Communist domination in the union was being challenged.

Accusations of ballot rigging in the Electrical Trades Union, the most important under complete Communist domination, became so frequent that in 1958 the T.U.C. General Council felt obliged to take the matter up. 'The General Council,' records their annual report, 'though unwilling to appear to be unduly influenced by large-scale press propaganda, were nevertheless agreed that allegations of the manipulation of elections in the E.T.U. and comment about the influence of the Communist Party in the affairs of that union were so widespread and persistent that it was becoming increasingly difficult for the General Council to ignore the effect of them on the prestige and public reputation of the trade union movement as a whole. The General Council, therefore, decided to write to the E.T.U. calling the attention of its executive council to and asking for its comments upon the observations made publicly about elections in the E.T.U. and the extent to which the union's affairs were influenced or controlled by the Communist Party.'

That was in December 1958. A long drawn out correspondence followed, with the E.T.U. leaving their reply until the last moment on every occasion. The General Council pressed them particularly on the question of taking legal proceedings against newspapers and journals which had specifically accused the union or its principal officers of manipulating elections. The union said such a course would merely provide a propaganda platform from which attacks could be continued.

There was a long hold-up in the correspondence while the E.T.U. conducted their own investigation and exonerated themselves from all blame. The T.U.C. were not satisfied with that and in the autumn of 1959 summoned the union executive to meet their Finance and General Purposes Committee.

When the E.T.U. leaders again put them off, the General Council lost patience. 'In view of the evasive nature of the replies sent by the union's leadership in answer to the comparatively simple questions put to them by the General Council,' they announced, 'and their persistent habit of seeking to delay the General Council in reaching a conclusion, the General Council do not propose to engage in any further abortive discussions of this character with the present E.T.U. leadership either by letters to the union's general secretary or through meetings with the union's representatives.

'Indeed, the General Council have come quite firmly to the conclusion that the principal reason why the present E.T.U. leadership has consistently sought to evade and to delay dealing with the charges publicly made against them and which the General Council brought to their notice, is because the present E.T.U. leadership, who are in a position to know, are aware that there is so much substance in these charges that they are unwilling to have them thoroughly investigated and unable specifically and unequivocally to deny them.'

They added that they would inform all affiliated unions of their decision and of the reasons for it.

If the General Council thought that would end the matter they were mistaken. That autumn Mr Frank Foulkes, the Communist president, was re-elected for another five-year term, though with a greatly reduced majority of about 3000. And in February 1960, after a bitterly contested election, the general secretary, Mr Frank Haxell, a member of the Communist Party executive, was declared re-elected by 1034 votes. But the votes of about 100 of the 700 branches were disallowed. Accusations of malpractice were redoubled. Opponents of the leadership in the union declared that if the votes of those branches had been counted Mr Haxell would have been easily defeated. There was a storm of protest in the Press, and the B.B.C. brought members of the union to the television screen to accuse the Communist leadership of election frauds.

The T.U.C. General Council could not keep their vow of silence. At their February 1960 meeting they summoned E.T.U. reresentatives to meet their Finance and General Purposes Committee on the grounds that the union's failure to counter the accusations was detrimental to the interests of the trade union movement. At their next meeting the General Council gave the E.T.U. a month to decide between suing people who have accused them of malpractice or accepting an independent inquiry into the allegations.

There was a further delay of a month because of the threat of legal action against the union by one of its members, Mr Cannon. The T.U.C. then gave the E.T.U. until 18 May to inform them of their decision, on pain of suspension from membership of the T.U.C.

The E.T.U. on 17 May agreed to the suggestion of an inquiry provided it was conducted by someone in sympathy with the aims and objects of the trade union movement, not some 'judicial' person not connected with the movement. They said, however, that they could not agree to the inquiry taking place while the union was facing legal proceedings, and to the last point the General Council agreed, for by then two members of the union had begun legal proceedings against the union and its leaders.

The plaintiffs were Mr John Byrne, a Scottish area official who was the unsuccessful candidate when Mr Haxell was re-elected, and Mr Frank Chapple, an anti-Communist member of the executive. They sought a declaration either that Mr Byrne was validly elected general secretary or that a new election should be held under safeguards decided by the Court. Mr Byrne also sought damages for conspiracy.

Heard in the High Court in the spring of 1961, the case lasted thirty-eight days and was said to have cost £80,000. It may well become a landmark in trade union history, for the result confirmed the allegations that had been made against the union leaders over a period of many years. Mr Justice Winn, in his judgement on 28 June, found that the union had been managed and controlled by the Communist party to serve its own ideals and that there was a conspiracy to prevent the election of Mr Byrne as general secretary, in which five of the defendants, including Mr Foulkes and Mr Haxell, were proved to have taken part. One result was a renewal in several newspapers of the demand that the Chief Registrar of Friendly Societies should be given greater powers of supervision over trade unions. Mr Justice Winn further directed that Mr Byrne was to assume the general secretaryship immediately, and that the defendant and the E.T.U. were to bear the costs of the case. At the time of writing an appeal by the defendants is pending.

The disqualification of branch votes was not the main cause of complaint in earlier elections. The allegation usually was that Communist-influenced branches falsified their returns. Many details of branch voting figures were published which made it difficult to believe that an honest return was made. It may be that there was some fiddling on the other side too, in an amateur, haphazard way, but the fiddling on the Communist side was said to have been carried out systematically in anything up to sixty branches. If they each gave only 100 additional votes to their candidate, that meant an extra 6000 votes, which would normally be decisive.

This kind of thing is possible partly because the majority of members are so little interested that they probably do not know an election is going on and certainly would not bother to ask for their voting paper. Even after all the propaganda of the previous year, only about sixteen per cent of the union membership recorded their votes in the Haxell election.

Unofficial strikes and left wing attacks on official leadership did not begin with the Communists and have not been confined to them. Since the British Communist Party was formed in 1920, however, they have cultivated and often succeeded in leading the rebellious left. It was part of Lenin's teaching that the party must work within the Labour movement but against the 'reformist' leaders. He argued that if they were eventually to seize power and establish the dictatorship of the proletariat then they must build

121

up a mass party. They could do that only by securing support where the masses of the workers were to be found, in the trade unions, the Labour Party, and the cooperatives. They were to form 'cells' everywhere and do their utmost to discredit the existing leaders and prepare for assumption of the leadership themselves.

It took some time for British Communists to replace the old tradition of loyalty to elected leaders by a policy of deliberately trying to discredit them, but eventually it was accepted and, as the Chapman incident illustrated, is now pursued without compunction.

In 1929, just over thirty years ago, the T.U.C. was warning trade unions against the disruptive activities of the Communist Party, and they have done so at intervals ever since.

From the early twenties until 1946, when a change of rule made it impossible, the Communists tried vainly to secure affiliation to the Labour Party. Deprived of official standing, their interests were pursued in the Labour Party by crypto-Communists (secret members) and fellow-travellers (who followed the Communist Party line without being members). The trouble they have thus caused has been constant but never very serious.

They have had more success in the trade unions, but it was a good many years before they began to make serious inroads into the movement. Failing to obtain substantial union support in their first years, they formed the National Minority Movement in 1924, which succeeded in capturing some trades councils for a time. In 1927 Moscow ordered a change of line to the 'class against class' policy, which meant attacking the Labour Party and splitting the trade unions rather than trying to work with them. They succeeded in forming one small breakaway union. This change destroyed what little they had achieved.

Following the rise of the Nazis in the early thirties the Communist International line was changed again and national parties were instructed to seek alliances with others in a 'united front' and later the 'popular front' against Fascism. In Britain they were successful in forming a propaganda alliance with the Independent Labour Party and Socialist League, led by Sir

Stafford Cripps. They also exploited the unemployed through the National Unemployed Workers' Movement. Their membership began to grow again, though it was still very small (less than 16,000 in 1938) and they made steady progress in the infiltration of the unions.

British Communists have always followed the twists of policy laid down in Moscow, though on several occasions they have got a twist behind. The classic example of that was their attitude to the Second World War. When it was first declared, they announced that it was an anti-Fascist war which everyone should support but their representative on the Communist International came hot-foot from Moscow to explain that they had got it wrong. So they promptly reversed their attitude, declaring the war to be an imperialist one and therefore to be opposed. But when Russia was invaded they had to change their line again, discovering that it was an anti-Fascist war after all.

The effect of the changes was mainly felt in the workshops. Before the invasion of Russia, they opposed efforts to increase production and fostered industrial trouble wherever they could. Afterwards they opposed strikes, fought for higher production, insisted on the necessity of national unity. Party membership rose to some 50,000.

This policy was continued for two years after the war. As late as August 1947, a Communist party booklet entitled *Looking Ahead* said: 'The Government should call on all workers associated with the key industries (including those producing their equipment and supplies) to work one week-end in four, at the appropriate overtime rates, as their special contribution to helping solve the production crisis in those industries. It should examine the possibilities of organizing great week-end volunteer brigades from all other industries to help in any way possible in the key industries.'

But they were once again behind the times. The Marshall Plan had already appeared and the cold was war on. In September 1947, the Communist Information Bureau (Cominform) was set up to fulfil the functions of the old Communist International, and within a few months the Communist Party were once more virulently attacking the official leadership and condemning 'cooperation with the master class'. Since then the struggle in the unions has been bitter and unceasing.

In the autumn of 1948 the T.U.C. General Council issued two statements, exposing Communist activities, which were later published as a pamphlet entitled *Defend Democracy*. They were satisfied, the Council said, that disruptive policies were being carried on by the Communist Party and its subsidiary organizations in 'servile obedience' to decisions made by the body calling itself the Cominform. They directed the attention of all trade unionists to the 'malignant character' of Communist agitation and organization.

The language of the General Council's denunciation was unrestrained. The Communists, they said, were 'acting as the abject and slavish agents of forces working incessantly to intensify social misery and to create conditions of chaos and economic instability'. Their most active and craftily planned arrangements operated inside the trade union movement. Such conspiratorial work had gone on for many years and had grown.

The General Council also expressed concern about Communist activities in certain trades councils, which bring together representatives of union branches in the localities. Communist and Fascist delegates had been banned from trades councils in 1934 but the ban was lifted in 1943, and they had since captured control of some of the largest trades councils, including those of London and Glasgow.

In January 1949, the T.U.C. and other Western trade union centres gave up the attempt to work with the Communists in the World Federation of Trade Unions and broke away from it to form later in the year the International Confederation of Free Trade Unions.

In March 1949, the General Council produced a new statement entitled *The Tactics of Disruption*. 'The leaders of the Communist parties', they said, 'have never regarded the trade union movement as a means of organizing workers either for the protection of those workers or to improve their standard of living. The so-called "intellectuals" of the Communist party regard the trade unions as instruments for the development of "mass struggle", to be used as a means of securing political power. Once political power is achieved, the independence of the unions is snatched away. They are rendered impotent to defend their members, and relegated to a position of subservience within the State, charged with the responsibility of unquestioningly obeying decisions made for them by the Communist party caucus.'

In 1955, the T.U.C. produced yet another pamphlet repeating their earlier denunciations.

After such fierce condemnation of Communists by the leaders of the trade union movement, it might have been supposed that trade unionists would stop electing Communists to high office. They did not do so. But the process of penetration had inevitably been protracted. Few trade union officials of any standing joined the Communist Party on its formation, and the journey to the top of the trade union hierarchy is a slow one from unpaid shop steward or branch official to minor paid positions and so by gradual stages to the top. By the beginning of the Second World War, Communists held a considerable number of intermediate positions in several unions, and during and after the war they began seriously to challenge for the highest posts.

By 1948 their progress had been formidable. A survey in *The Times* that year recorded that they held four general secretary-ships – of the miners, electricians, foundrymen, and firemen. They had one member on the T.U.C. General Council, a lay representative of the Transport and General Workers' Union. Their representation was negligible on the executives of the builders' and printers' federations but substantial on that of the ship-building and engineering unions. It was also substantial on the General Council of the builders' federation, a larger body than the executive.

Of the fifteen unions with a membership of more than 100,000, it was indicated, the Communists and their supporters had sufficient representation on the executives to control or dispute control of four – the Electrical Trades Union, the Amalgamated Engineering Union, the Civil Service Clerical Association, and the Tailors' and Garment Workers' Union, while they had appreciable influence on six – the Transport and General Workers', the Miners', the Railwaymen's, the Distributive Workers', the Teachers', and the Post Office Workers'. In the other five their influence was negligible.

Among smaller unions, they were said to have strong or appreciable influence in the Fire Brigades' Union, the Post Office Engineering Union, the Foundry Workers', the Cine-technicians', the Scientific Workers' and the Clerical and Administrative Workers'. They had little influence in any of the industries limited to particular industrial areas such as cotton, woollen textiles, boots and shoes, pottery, or hosiery.

The Communists had a majority on the London Trades Council and a number of other trades councils in various parts of the country. They also had control of an independent research organization, the Labour Research Department, to which many trade unions and branches were affiliated, and of the shop Stewards National Council.

Since then there have been a dozen years of continual struggle for power. Some unions acted in time to eliminate completely the Communist threat or to avert immediate danger. The Transport and General Workers' Union, at their conference in 1949, adopted a rule that no member of the Communist party should be eligible to hold office either as a lay member or as a full-time officer. This decision automatically removed the one Communist from the T.U.C. General Council, which remained free of them until September 1960, when Mr Will Paynter, general secretary of the National Union of Mineworkers, was elected. Communist activity in the T.G.W.U. has been largely confined to rank-and-file level, though recently some ex-Communists have been regaining influence in the passenger transport section.

The Clerical and Administrative Workers' Union adopted a rule that every candidate for office must state if he is a member of an organization proscribed by the Labour party and this seems to have been effective. The N.U.R. have since 1934 been bound by a conference resolution that the president, general secretary, and two assistant general secretaries must not be members of the Communist party or any organization proscribed by the Labour party. About a quarter of their executive in 1960 were believed to be Communists or supporters, however.

An active group of Labour party members in the Union of Shop, Distributive and Allied Workers reduced Communist influence to negligible proportions. An unofficial conference campaign committee succeeded in removing the danger in the Civil Service Clerical Association. The Communists monopolized the leadership in the Fire Brigades' Union for a time, but after the Hungarian uprising the general secretary, Mr John Horner, and other officials resigned from the party in a block.

At one time the Communists came near to capturing the Amalgamated Society of Woodworkers. They were opposed by a small but active group. In 1949 a leading Communist in the union, Mr Norman Kennedy, resigned from the party and devoted great energy and skill to fighting his former comrades. He was killed in a car accident in 1954, but by then the danger had been staved off and it now looks as if the anti-Communists are holding their own.

In the Foundry Workers' Union, the former general secretary, Mr J. Gardner, was a Communist and the union, though there were no other party members on the executive, followed the party line religiously. They were challenged by a group of anti-Communists, who gained some surprising successes before Mr Gardner's retirement in 1958. The struggle is by no means over, however.

In 1948, the Communists were just consolidating their position in the Electrical Trades Union, having won the general secretaryship a little earlier. Once in power, there were many measures they could take to secure themselves and before long their domination appeared impregnable, though there remained a few non-Communist outposts, of which the most notable was Glasgow, where Mr Byrne, a Catholic, was the district secretary. The Soviet intervention in Hungary produced some resignations and resistance became more active. By 1960 there were three anti-Communists on the executive and the T.U.C. General Council were taking action, as has been described.

The most sustained and bitter battle of all has been in the Amalgamated Engineering Union, the second largest union in the country, with members in almost every industry. More than once the Communists have come close to gaining control of the seven-man executive, but at the time of writing they have only one member on it. The president and general secretary and two of the three national organizers are all non-Communists. Until recently all officers were elected for only three years – it is now five – so that the electoral struggle was continuous, though the proportion of members recording their votes was seldom as much as ten per cent.

The danger first became acute during the war. An anti-Communist organization was established at meetings of the fifty-two-member national committee, their ruling body, in 1943 and 1944, and was followed a few years later by a loose national organization, working in secret and known as 'the side' or the 'antis' which succeeded in removing a good many Communists from office. The anti-Communists are constantly at odds among themselves, however, and can seldom agree on one candidate for a office, as the Communists always do. This is not necessarily fatal, as, if no candidate gets an overall majority on the first poll, then the two with the highest votes go forward to a final vote, but it is always a disadvantage.

In the last few years the struggle has been given increased publicity in the Press and on radio and television – a factor which has played an important part in the penetration into the Communist strongholds in Sheffield and north London. Another important factor has been the strong leadership of Mr William Carron since he was elected president in 1956.

The position in the National Union of Mineworkers continues to cause non-Communists some anxiety. The Communists have always had a minority of only six or seven in the twenty-eight-man executive, but twice since the war the union has elected a Communist as general secretary. In the Scottish area they have established a control as complete as they exercised in the Electrical Trade Union. The exposure of Stalin and the suppression of the Hungarian uprising resulted in some important resignations from the party, for instance by Mr Wynne the Derbyshire leader and Mr Allen in Northumberland, but the only anti-Communist gains seem to have been by resignations. The Communists have strengthened their position in south Wales, where they now have the president and general secretary, as well as nearly half the executive. They have also strengthened their position in parts of the Yorkshire coalfield. The policy of the union has been moving steadily to the left.

Apart from the individual unions, the Communists have made little impression on the federations. Communist-controlled trades councils in London, Glasgow, and elsewhere were disbanded by the T.U.C. and new councils set up in their place. A new system of registration makes it possible for the T.U.C. to maintain a continuous watch on their activities.

Taking the movement as a whole, it is probably fair to say that in the past twelve years the Communist offensive has been halted and that they have been forced back on important sections of the front, even though the resignations which followed the exposure of Stalin and the Hungarian revolt may not all have resulted from a real change of heart. They did result in increased Trotskyist activity in rivalry with the Communists.

There are still far more Communists in important positions in the unions than can be explained by the number of Communist trade union members. The whole membership of the party had fallen by 1958 to 25,000, while there are 9,600,000 trade unionists. Even if the fellow-travellers are added, the Communists must be fewer than a half of one per cent of the membership. It has been estimated that there are fewer than 300 Communist party members and perhaps twice that number of fellow-travellers in the 230,000-strong Electrical Trades Union.

It is sometimes said that Communists drive members away from union meetings by the tedious multiplication of resolutions on the party line. On the other hand it has been argued that, by providing a live opposition, they prevent members from becoming even more apathetic than they are and act as a check on tendencies to bureaucracy.

They damage the unions because their primary concern is to forward the interests not of the members, except possibly in a vague long-term sort of way, but of the Soviet Union, which they regard as the standard-bearer of the emancipation of the workers of the world from the bonds of capitalism. They damage the unions even more because, while they are constantly spreading and prolonging strikes, and advocating unreasonable wage demands, it is very hard for their non-Communist opponents to give the unions intelligent leadership. There is pressure on them all the time to try to rival the Communists in militancy to secure the support of their members.

7

POWER ABUSED

Vitriol and Bombs – Bludgeoning the Blackleg –
Penalizing the Poacher – Banning the Breakaway – The Solid Block

*There shall none come into the town to serve for that wages within
a twelve month and a day, but we woll have an harme or a legge of
hym, except they woll take an othe as we have doon* – Journeymen
shoemakers of Wisbech claiming a wage increase from master
shoemakers, as reported by the Bishop of Ely to Thomas Crom-
well in 1538.

*The means which are used by this destructive combination are just
as atrocious as the object. Not only the masters but the industrious
workmen must obey its orders . . . if they wish to avoid being
murdered or excoriated with vitriol. . . . Many living and melancholy
proofs of it* (the use of vitriol) *are now lingering in their beds or
pining through the streets blind and disfigured, rendered for life
equally burdensome to themselves and to the community* – Henry
Houldsworth, cotton manufacturer and magistrate, writing to
Robert Peel, Home Secretary, from Glasgow in 1823.

*Recalcitrant workmen were terrorized by explosions of cans of
gunpowder in the troughs of their grinding wheels, or thrown down
their chimneys; and in some cases these explosions caused serious
injury* – Sidney and Beatrice Webb, in their *History of Trade
Unionism*, describing the Sheffield outrages of the 1860s.

Compared with the savage reprisals of past times, the sending
of blacklegs to Coventry, which has aroused so much indignation
in recent years, is civilized. Like the outrages quoted, the practice
is exceptional, the outcome of failure by a few men to restrain the
promptings of a deep-rooted anger and fear. In the industrial
struggle, the worker's only basic weapon is his power to withdraw his labour in concert with his comrades. The blacklegs
strike at the root of that power. They are to the trade union
movement what traitors are to a nation in time of war.

131

The detestation of blackleg and scab is perhaps the most deeply rooted of all trade union instincts. When strikes meant suffering and hunger, and sometimes persecution, for men and their families, it was not surprising that they sometimes gave way to violence. Strikes now result in financial loss and deprivation of comforts, and it is not surprising that men sometimes refuse to speak to fellow-workers who let them down. Social ostracism was not invented by the unions and it is no new thing for traitors to be exposed to it.

To explain that kind of primitive action is not to justify it. The unions have the power to impose disciplinary penalties on those who fail to carry out instructions issued according to rule. Workers can hardly be expected to feel friendly to blacklegs, but that does not mean there is reason to impose additional social penalties.

We have been speaking of action against men who go to work during a strike called by their union. Public revulsion has been particularly and justifiably aroused by the sending to Coventry of men and women who have refused to take part in unofficial strikes, of which there have been a number of instances. Such men are victimized by their own comrades for loyalty to their union rules. Some of the 'little Napoleons' described in Chapter 4 have shown a shocking vindictiveness in carrying out and prolonging punishment. One man was reported to have felt the ostracism so deeply that he committed suicide, though other factors probably contributed to his state of mind at the time.

In certain circumstances the victim of persecution can get the protection of the courts. There was a fitter and turner named Huntley at Gray's shipyard in Hartlepool who refused to take part in the one-day national strike called by the Confederation of Shipbuilding and Engineering Unions in December 1953. His employers refused to sack him, and he was sent to Coventry. When summoned before the Hartlepool district committee of the Amalgamated Engineering Union, he described them collectively as a 'shower'. The committee asked for his expulsion, but the national executive repeatedly turned them down.

Huntley got a job in Bradford but soon returned. The committee prevented him from getting work in Hartlepool and when he was given employment at a power station at Stockton, union officials got him dismissed by threatening to call a strike. His union subscriptions were refused and then he was expelled for being in arrears. He sued for damages and got £500.

The fear of being treated as a blackleg has much to do with support for unofficial strikes. Without any formal decision by a committee, the disapproval of his workmates can make life unpleasant not only for the man himself but also for his family. Obviously fear of such treatment is particularly strong in closely knit communities such as those of the miners and dockers.

To many of those taking part in unofficial strikes, the man carrying out his union's rules by remaining at work is no different from any other blackleg. He has let them down when they are engaged in a fight. They do not appreciate the wider loyalty. But union executives have often reinstated men penalized or expelled for not taking part in an unofficial strike.

Sending men to Coventry has, of course, no place in the rules or policy of any union. Union leaders have on occasion condemned the practice in strong terms, but because they do not speak out often enough in public they tend to create the impression that they are condoning it by their silence. When they do speak, it is in general terms. Seldom do they criticize a particular action. No doubt they are reluctant to join in public attacks, which may be exaggerated and misconceived, and many do their best in a quiet way to eliminate such things in their own organizations, but no disciplinary action has been taken, so far as is known, against branches which impose such penalties.

Blacklegging is the unforgivable sin in the trade union creed, but there are others. A serious crime, in certain circumstances, is to work too hard. The instances of punishments for such offences are rare but curious. There was a milkman who was fined £2 for delivering milk too early in the morning, a plumber who was reproved for using a bicycle to get to his jobs, a factory inspector who caused a sit-down strike by not taking his second week's holiday. The attitude is understandable. Hard-won concessions are endangered if workers do not take advantage of them.

Regular and systematic limitation of output is a different matter, but does not seem to be prevalent.

One of the most extraordinary cases of this kind was the strike in 1955 at the Rolls-Royce factory at Blantyre, in Scotland. Mr Joseph McLernon, a polisher, was accused by those working with him of breaking an agreement to restrict bonus earnings because there was a temporary shortage of work. The exact facts were in dispute, but after prolonged argument he was expelled from his union, the General Iron Fitters' Association. The shop stewards, with Communists prominent among them, then demanded his dismissal on the grounds that he was a non-unionist, but the firm refused. The polishers went on strike; before long the whole factory was out, and the dispute had spread to two neighbouring factories at Hillington and East Kilbride.

Altogether 7500 men ceased work, and several unions, including the Iron Fitters', the Electrical Trades Union, and the Amalgamated Engineering Union, gave the strike official backing. The strike lasted seven weeks – in the Christmas period – but eventually collapsed. McLernon was a Roman Catholic and after the strike had failed Roman Catholics conducted an anti-Communist campaign. But a week or two later the workers at the Hillington factory re-elected their Communist convener of shop stewards by a large majority.

Strikes against the employment of non-unionists are not infrequent when unions are trying to establish or maintain a closed shop. Union strength depends on holding their ranks solid and keeping discipline, which inevitably results in restrictions on individual freedom, as the rules of any organization must restrict the freedom of those who join it. Disciplinary action can result in disproportionate hardship when a union maintains a closed shop, however.

Instances of this have resulted in complaints that unions are repressive of individual liberty. There has been talk of the 'right' of a worker not to join a union or 'to join the union of his choice'. A good deal of loose thinking is to be found in these complaints, but they are not baseless.

Public attention was focused on the closed shop issue in 1955 by the Bonsor case. Mr Bonsor was expelled from the Musicians' Union in 1949 on the grounds that he was in arrears in his subscriptions. Without a union card, he was unable to follow his calling as a musician and worked at various times as a labourer, assistant cook, porter, waiter, and chipping rust off a Brighton pier. Meanwhile he fought a legal action against the union to regain membership and get damages for loss of earnings. In 1953 the High Court ruled that his expulsion was null and void, because it had not been carried out in accordance with the rules of the union, but dismissed his case for damages and the Court of Appeal upheld this decision. Meanwhile Mr Bonsor had died, but his widow took the case to the House of Lords, who allowed the appeal and ordered the case back to the High Court to assess damages.

The judgement established for the first time the right to damages in this type of case, but it depended on the fact that the rules of the union were not exactly followed when Mr Bonsor was expelled. If they had been he would have been deprived of his normal livelihood and would have had no redress. A union cannot be expected to keep in membership a man who fails to pay his contributions, but it was widely felt that the union's power over the individual is so great that he should have some right of appeal to an independent authority, or alternatively that the closed shop should be outlawed.

The T.U.C. attitude to the closed shop was set out at the 1946 congress at Brighton. It should be explained that the term 'closed shop' is here used in the loose connotation usual in Britain to indicate any undertaking where every worker is compelled, either by union action or by the employers, to belong to a recognized union. The technical differences between the closed shop and the union shop and their variations, which are well understood in the United States where they are much commoner, need not concern us, but the T.U.C. preferred to describe their aim as the '100 per cent union shop' to make it clear that they do not necessarily seek that all the workers in an undertaking should be organized in *one* union.

The subject was arousing controversy in 1946 because members of the Transport and General Workers' Union on London buses had refused to work with members of the National Passenger Workers' Union, an organization claiming 4000 members which broke away from the T.G.W.U. after the London bus strike of 1937. The London Passenger Transport Board had consequently decided to make membership of the T.G.W.U. a condition of employment in the grades it covered. About the same time T.G.W.U. members in Smithfield market were threatening to strike against the employment of non-unionists and of members of the Smithfield Guild of Clerks and Salesmen, and a number of local authorities, freed to do so by the repeal of the Trade Disputes Act, were making membership of a recognized union a condition of employment.

Regarding the liberty of the individual, the T.U.C. laid down their policy as follows: 'The position of the non-unionist cannot be justified on grounds either of principle or of expediency. The liberty of the individual is not an absolute and unqualified right. It is subject to restrictions for social ends which admit of no compromise, and one of them is that the presence of non-unionists may result, and often has resulted in the past, in the stoppage of an entire trade. Stability, order, and regularity in the conduct of industry depend upon the proper functioning of trade unions, and upon the recognition of the fact that no man or woman is entitled to benefit from the work of trade unions without acceptance of the obligations of trade union membership. . . . Recognition of such obligations is incumbent not only upon individual workers but upon managements and employers.'

In a later passage they say: 'A union which has the responsibility of maintaining fair wages and working conditions must also have the right to determine, according to the circumstances in the particular case, whether or not it is wise or safe to tolerate non-unionism and thereby permit the presence of actual or potential blacklegs, in industries where union rates and conditions have been established.'

The closed shop exists only in a few sections of British industry. The craft unions used to impose it more strongly than they do, but some of them still exercise effective control in printing, shipbuilding, cotton, and parts of the engineering industry. It is often to be found among unions generally on the docks, in the mines, in London Transport, in the London markets, in Cooperative Societies, in music and films, and in numerous individual firms.

Few local authorities have attempted to enforce it, and where they have done so have sometimes been resisted by such trade unions as those of teachers and other white-collar workers. The comparatively low percentage of trade unionists in most industries shows that the closed shop cannot be widespread.

The issue has seldom arisen in a major way since 1946, except through instances of individual persecution, of which the Bonsor case is the most notable. Strikes against the employment of non-unionists in individual firms, for instance in the motor industry, have not been uncommon. They have usually been the result either of a provocative attitude on the part of the non-unionist or of the desire of some little Napoleon to find a pretext for strife.

In 1959, the National Union of Railwaymen asked the British Transport Commission to make union membership a condition of employment and withdrew from the consultative machinery when their request was refused. By the end of the year, however, they had compromised on a statement by the Commission encouraging employees to join a union. Such encouragement is given in many industries and firms where there is no closed shop.

The other main 'individual freedom' issue, the 'right' of a worker to join the union of his choice, was also dealt with in the T.U.C. report. It arises when the movement takes action against a breakaway union or against a union which is held to have poached members from another. In one case, the movement attempts to destroy a union which workers have formed and to which they prefer to belong, as it destroyed the National Passenger Workers' Union. In the other, operating the Bridlington agreement, it orders the poacher to return the members poached. Critics have found it repugnant that workers should be compelled to give up their union or be moved from one union to another through no fault of their own and without having any say in the matter or any appeal.

If they are dissatisfied with their own union, it is suggested, they should have the right to leave it for another. In fact they have, if they carry out the conditions laid down in the Bridlington agreement, and if there is another suitable union operating in the place where they work. But if there is only one union operating there, they have no escape, however dissatisfied they may be with it. It is frequently pointed out that where membership is compulsory, and where there is no competing organization, there is little incentive to a union to give its members a good service or to carry out their wishes.

One of the most depressing post-war stories has been that of the Aeronautical Engineers Association, which has been treated as a breakaway union though it was not so in origin. The association was formed in April 1943, by civilian aircraft maintenance men employed by the Air Ministry, most of them men from Government training centres who felt they were being unjustly treated by a new merit pay scheme as compared with those who by apprenticeship or otherwise were entitled to join the Amalgamated Engineering Union as skilled men.

From the first they were treated with enmity by the other unions, particularly the A.E.U. and the Transport and General Workers' Union. They were refused recognition by the Air Ministry, though they had more than 2000 members, with a substantial majority in some shops, and though their claim to include a high proportion of fully skilled men, many of them more skilled than some A.E.U. members, appears to have been justified.

Since then they have repeatedly sought recognition from Government Ministers, Labour and Conservative, and the air corporations. They have several times applied for affiliation to the T.U.C. They have attempted to take their claims to arbitration and to courts of law. They have even appealed to the International Labour Organization. They have several times threatened to strike. Their case has been taken up by Members of Parliament and questions have been asked in the House. It has all been fruitless.

Their membership has naturally dwindled, but the loyalty of most of their members, through nearly twenty years without recognition, and in spite of constant attacks and attempts at coercion by other unions in the airports, has been astonishing. In 1957 they claimed still to have 1200 members and were complaining of discrimination against them in B.O.A.C. promotion policy.

In an attempt to secure affiliation to the T.U.C., they agreed to merge with the National Engineers' Association, a small affiliated union. The T.U.C. promptly expelled the N.E.A. and the merger was not carried through.

The conduct of the Ae.E.A. has in some respects been misguided. They made a fatal blunder in 1946 when they joined with the National Passenger Workers' Union to form the short-lived Federation or Independent Trade Unions. The federation claimed at one time to have brought together forty-five non-T.U.C. unions with a combined membership of some 400,000, but actual membership never approached those figures. Without the support of the two main non-T.U.C. unions, the National and Local Government Officers' Association and the National Union of Teachers, they could get nowhere and the only result was to arouse the lasting resentment of the T.U.C.

The Ae.E.A. may have mismanaged a good case, in very difficult circumstances. They would have been well advised to have accepted one of the offers of amalgamation made to them by the big unions. But they were treated vindictively by the other unions and the attitude towards their members of Labour and Conservative Governments, the air corporations, and the T.U.C., based on fear of offending the A.E.U. and the T.G.W.U., seems to have been contemptible.

Long, vain struggles for recognition have also taken place among unions in the Civil Service, several of which joined the Federation of Independent Trade Unions.

In the Post Office recognition was formerly governed by the 'Listowel Formula' which said that where an association had in membership at least forty per cent of the organized staff in the grade or grades concerned, recognition would be granted for an initial period of three years. If after that membership fell below $33\frac{1}{2}$ per cent, the question of withdrawal of recognition would arise. It was also a recognized principle, not always carried out in practice, that not more than one association should be recognized as representing classes whose members had substantially identical interests. There were thirty-one unions recognized by the Post Office.

In 1952 a committee under the chairmanship of Lord Terrington, set up by the Postmaster General to examine the problem, recommended the abolition of the Listowel Formula, with no other percentage formula to take its place. Other recommendations were that there should not be more than one union representing a grade or group of grades, that the Post Office should re-examine all cases of dual recognition, that an association claiming recognition should be required to prove that the existing recognized association had failed and was unable to look after the interests of those concerned, and that the claiming body must be financially stable and so organized that it could serve its members better than the existing recognized organization. They also recommended that recognition should not be granted on the basis of sex and that facilities to organize should not be granted to an unrecognized association. Such stringent conditions clearly made it practically impossible for any new organization to achieve recognition.

The committee applied their new principles to the claims of seven unions, and advocated recognition of only one very small one, with an accompanying suggestion that they should seek amalgamation with a larger union. The Engineering Officers' (Telecommunications) Association was one whose claims had received frequent attention in Parliament and elsewhere. Conservatives actually forced a vote in the House when they were in opposition but the Conservative Government refused recognition when in office. Eventually they took their 5000 members into the Post Office Engineering Union in 1954.

The principles of the Terrington report do not seem to have been adopted by the Civil Service generally, where recognition depends on representing a considerable proportion of the grades concerned, without any fixed percentage. Several unrecognized unions have disappeared and the issue is no longer a live one.

Another long-established unrecognized union in outside industry, with a sizeable membership, is the Union of Railway Signalmen, which keeps up the fight against the National Union of

Railwaymen year after year, and in 1952 claimed to have survived the biggest-ever campaign against it with 180 working branches. Another is the Gas Industrial Union which, as its name implies, believes that the interests of gas workers would be better served by an industrial union than by membership of a general union. Most gas workers are in the National Union of General and Municipal Workers.

The claims of most of the rebel unions is that they represent special classes of workers whose interests are not adequately safeguarded by the larger unions. There are strong arguments, however, against increasing the number of unions, with all the confusion and difficulties in negotiation which result from the existence of rival and competing organizations.

Cases of 'poaching', often unintentional, are quite common. As was pointed out in Chapter 3, every year the Disputes Committees of the T.U.C. order several unions to 'return' or 'cease to take contributions from' members they were held to have recruited wrongfully.

In 1955 and 1956, however, union members caused some consternation in the T.U.C. by appealing to the courts against their exclusion from an offending union. The first was a case in which the T.U.C. had ordered the National Union of Public Employees to expel seven Truro ambulance staff on the grounds that they had been poached. One of the seven, Mr R. H. Andrew, obtained an injunction to prevent the union from expelling him on the grounds that there was nothing in the union's rules which provided for expulsion at the behest of the T.U.C.

The case which attracted most public attention, however, was that of Mr Francis Spring, one of anything up to 10,000 men 'poached' by the National Amalgamated Stevedores and Dockers from the Transport and General Workers' Union in Hull, Liverpool, Birkenhead, and Manchester. Mr Spring obtained a decision from the Chancery Court at Liverpool that his expulsion was illegal. The N.A.S.D. was compelled to keep the poached members and to provide them with normal union services though they had failed, in spite of their long strike in 1955, to obtain negotiating rights for them.

The T.U.C. were faced with a break-down in their machinery for preventing unrestricted competition between unions in accordance with the Bridlington agreement. Some prophesied a chaotic position in union organization resulting in widespread industrial disputes, but in the event things went on much as before.

The T.U.C., after long consideration, decided at that year's Congress to ask unions to alter their rules to enable them to expel members on the instructions of a T.U.C. disputes committee. By 1959, forty had done so and eighteen more were satisfied their existing rules were adequate. Others were preparing to take similar action.

In 1959 the N.A.S.D. was expelled from the T.U.C. for failing to carry out the instructions of the disputes committee, in spite of its plea that it was prevented by law from doing so. So it still has members in the northern ports, though fewer than at first. A good many dockers seem to have taken advantage of the position to drop out of both unions.

The issue raised by these developments was whether, if thousands of men were so dissatisfied with their own union that they joined another, they should not be allowed to remain in the new union and be given the representative rights their numbers warranted.

The issue was discussed in the General Council's interim report on structure and closer unity in 1944. 'It has often been argued', the report said, 'that any individual should have the right to choose to which union he desires to belong. As a general principle this appears to be sound, but we are striving to secure stability of trade union membership, coordination of effort, and the abolition of unnecessary competition. A handful of disgruntled members, having fully exploited the services of their union, may feel that membership of another union would suit them better. That feeling may be justified or otherwise, but the complete recognition of the right of members to move from union to union may destroy stability of organization, undermine loyalty, and lead to an undesirable extension of the number of unions concerned in negotiations with a single employer. Any union facilitating this chopping and changing would probably find that in their turn they would experience the same difficulties as the original union.'

Commenting on this, the 1946 report quoted earlier on says: 'Whilst no one would dispute in principle the right of freedom of the individual, if there were complete freedom to remain outside the union, or even to move at will from one union to another, we should have a trade union movement whose authority was completely undermined. The movement would then be an open target for critics who take every opportunity at the present time to complain of lack of discipline, and who, when unofficial strikes occur, allege that the unions cannot control their members. Moreover, such critics cannot on the one hand insist on the freedom of a worker to stay outside a union or to join any union he likes, without at the same time according to members of a *bona fide* union the freedom to decline to work with either non-unionists or members of a dissident union.'

Complaints of abuse of power are often made in relation to the use of the union block vote at the Trades Union Congress and the annual conference of the Labour party. This is the system by which each union casts a vote for the whole of its membership on one side, however much its membership may in fact be divided. A few of the biggest unions, acting together, can thus dominate the congress and conference, as happened during the rule of the Deakin–Lawther–Williamson triumvirate. Candidates for the T.U.C. General Council, and for the office of Labour party treasurer, and for the trade union or women's sections of the National Executive, knew that they could not hope for election if they had aroused the antipathy of the big unions.

The block votes have, in fact, been used to keep able but unapproved men off the General Council. Year after year the block votes were used against Mr Arthur Horner, the secretary of the National Union of Mineworkers, because he was a Communist (though his own union nominated and voted for him). Year after year they were used against Mr Len White, the brilliant but left-wing secretary of the Civil Service Clerical Association. Year after year they are used against Mr Bryn Roberts, general secretary of the National Union of Public Employees, the spectacular

143

rise of which in the past twenty-five years has not taken place without giving offence to the big general unions. Other examples could be quoted in which mediocrities have been preferred to able leaders.

It is generally believed that there is an understanding among the biggest unions that they will normally support each others candidates.

There was a remarkable example of this in 1958 when a 'caretaker' representative from the Woodworkers' union was elected to the General Council to keep the position open until the union had elected a new general secretary, and thus kept off the general secretary of the furniture workers, who had been a candidate for many years but was out of favour. Fear of new ideas and unconventional personalities seems to inspire many of the choices.

In the same way, at the Labour party conference, the block votes were used to restore Mr Herbert Morrison to the executive after he had been defeated in the constituency section. At one time it was intended to remove Arthur Greenwood from the position of treasurer to let Morrison in, but feeling against that was too strong so Mr Morrison was restored by making the Deputy Leader of the party an ex-officio member.

The block votes were also used to make Mr Gaitskell treasurer and to keep the more independent characters off the womens' section. There was the case of Mrs Eirene White, who withdrew her nomination, after she had offended the Transport and General Workers' Union, and made a public protest. In the trade union section, Mr Mark Hewitson was displaced by his own union because he fell out of step.

Complaints from the left wing were fewer after the triumvirate broke up, and the balance of block votes became more even, but the right wing suddenly discovered the injustice of the system when Mr Frank Cousins, with the aid of the block votes of his own and other unions, defeated the party leadership on nuclear disarmament at the 1960 conference.

8

DESCENDANTS OF KING LUDD

Impedimenta – Unmanned Printers – Absent Miners –
Demarcated Builders – Up With Output!

IN 1811 and 1812 the stockingers of Nottinghamshire and Leicestershire, the handloom weavers of Lancashire, and the cutters of Yorkshire took part in a series of riots in which they wrecked machines which were depriving them of their living, sometimes burnt mills, and even in some cases murdered millowners whose defenders shot them down. Their orders came to them secretly in the name of a legendary figure, Ned Ludd, or 'King Ludd', as he was often called, who was said to have his headquarters in Sherwood Forest.

The machine-wreckers were out again in 1815 and 1826. Their riots were suppressed with a savagery which today causes more revulsion than the wrecking of machines, but the name Luddite remains a term of opprobrium, applied to men who try violently to prevent the march of progress, as indeed they did. But it must be remembered that these men and their wives were near to starvation – 'meagre with famine, sullen with despair, careless of a life which your Lordships are perhaps about to value at something less than the price of a stocking-frame', as Lord Byron said in the House of Lords in vain opposition to a Bill to make frame-breaking a capital offence.

There were no trade unions able adequately to protect their interests, because trade unions were illegal and penalties for combinations were severe. There was no Labour party to put their case in Parliament, only a few isolated individuals who could do nothing against a frightened and vindictive Government. The Luddites, bewildered and alone, fought their battle for survival in the only way they could find.

The workers of today who fight against the march of progress have no such excuses. Nor do they smash machines. But they do impose restrictions, and some of these restrictions have the same object as the wrecking of machines by the Luddites – increasing the amount of labour required to produce a certain amount of output by preventing or limiting the use of the most efficient machines or methods. Some are intended less to increase the total amount of labour than to ensure that the work shall go to a particular class of worker. Others are to enable workers to maintain particular social habits and traditions or simply to make work lighter and more congenial. A good many of them became ossified during the period of high unemployment between the wars and have been difficult to move in the different economic circumstances of the post-war world.

Many union leaders will tell you that they know of no restrictive practices, only protective practices, designed to prevent exploitation of workers by excessive speed-up, or overtime, or the dangerous under-manning of machines, or inadequate rest periods, and to maintain good standards of work, of safety, and of health. A reasonable defence can be put up in many cases.

The prevalence of restrictive practices is very hard to estimate. Apart from the difficulty of deciding what practices are restrictive, many employers, conscious that their competitors are in the same position as themselves, would rather leave such things alone than run the risk of stirring up trouble. Many such practices are embodied in negotiated agreements, many are long-established customs.

There are numerous industries in which they are not regarded as a problem, but there are undoubtedly a few, including some important ones, in which they seriously impede efficiency. The subject was investigated by the Minister of Labour's National Joint Advisory Council after the passing of the Restrictive Trade Practices Act of 1956, to deal with employers' restrictions, had led to renewed demands that action should be taken to stop labour restrictions.

Before the N.J.A.C. got down to it, the British Employers' Confederation circularized their own member federations to obtain information. Of sixty-three organizations, twenty-two sent replies. Seven said they had no restrictive labour practices to speak of, four that there were only minor restrictions. These replies are perhaps of particular significance, since they were sent in confidence to their own confederation. Presumably most of those who did not reply had little to complain of.

Of the eleven which gave detailed replies, nine mentioned demarcation restrictions of various kinds. Though we have already discussed demarcation in another context, the summary of the employers' complaints can usefully be included here.

Some demarcation took the form of insistence that certain work must be done by particular classes of craftsmen, or by members of particular trade unions, irrespective of whether it could be efficiently performed by other craftsmen more readily available. In one industry there were said to be two or more classes of tradesmen equally competent to do a particular piece of work. Often compromise arrangements had to be made under which one class of craftsman did part of the work and another completed it, or a demarcation was made on the basis of the size or thickness of the materials, though this might be less efficient than one class doing the job.

Another form of demarcation restriction was insistence by some unions that their members should be employed on jobs that could equally well be done by semi-skilled or unskilled workers or women. One federation said that when new machinery or alteration of methods made certain work suitable for unskilled or semi-skilled men, there was the greatest reluctance on the part of the men who previously did it to recognize that their skill was being wasted. They insisted on pay on a skilled basis for work which no longer required their training, knowledge, and experience.

In another large industry, some repetitive processes had been developed which required some aptitude and training but not a craftsman's skill. The non-craft unions asked for special pay for such work, and the employers recognized that it was worth more than the labourers' rate. But some craft unions would not negotiate – or even discuss – semi-skilled rates of wages, insisting on two rates only, one for craftsmen and one for labourers.

Another federation said the unions insisted that the major part of the industry's productive work must be done by fully skilled

147

men on craftsmen's rates, although skilled men were very scarce. This tended to exclude semi-skilled and unskilled workers. It seriously limited output and increased costs.

One small but strong union insisted, it was said, on irritating job distinctions, for instance that men must be employed on certain light work done elsewhere by women, which put employers in the chief centre of the trade at a serious disadvantage against competitors in other districts.

Another aspect of demarcation, mentioned in several replies, was that some unions would not allow their members to perform any jobs outside their own trade, or even help in cases of emergency. They just had to wait for another worker whose job it was to do that kind of work. For instance, if a labourer was not there to draw materials for a skilled man, he remained idle until a labourer was available.

On some types of skilled work, such as the removal of a particular type of rubbish, a particular class of unskilled worker had to be employed. Another union representing skilled craftsmen in the same industry insisted that one of their members had to be called – if necessary from some other part of the premises – to do such jobs as switching on and off electric lights. Chargehands of one craft were not allowed to give instructions to general labourers of another craft, even in the same union.

In some of the industries demarcation provisions were laid down in agreements, but in most the restrictions were imposed by trade union rules, policy, or custom.

After demarcation, restrictions on overtime were most frequently mentioned. They were usually embodied in agreements, and some federations thought the agreed conditions unduly severe. Others said that in some localities unions or their members imposed restrictions outside the agreements. For instance, day-shift overtime would not be worked unless week-end overtime on higher rates was also provided. Or there was insistence that a specified minimum number of men must be employed on overtime if a single man was wanted, or that if overtime was required for one class of workers it should be provided for another class as well, even if that was unnecessary. Another federation said that since the introduction of the five-day week, the unions rigidly refused to permit overtime on Saturday mornings, even in a crisis. Several federations regarded some restriction on overtime as reasonable and a matter for negotiation.

Another frequently mentioned restriction was on the number of apprentices, sometimes laid down in agreements and sometimes imposed by the union. In certain industries this had resulted in shortages of skilled labour. Union practice might vary in different districts.

The next group of restrictions involved resistance to scientific work-load assessment and to schemes of redeployment of labour and machinery.

One federation laid emphasis on resistance to the introduction of time-study. Some of the unions had refused to recognize that work-loads can be scientifically assessed within a comparatively small margin of error, with the result that the existing lists of piece-work rates were riddled with anomalies whereby operatives received widely differing wages for similar work, and some were much more heavily loaded than others. This affected production adversely as it created bottlenecks and unpopular jobs while workers in other jobs had an easy time. Another result was that the unions often attempted to secure an undue share of the advantages of new machinery or improved appliances. This had been done either by insisting on the retention of the same or nearly the same number of machines per operative, thus reducing the work-load, or by accepting an increased number of machines per operative but claiming the same payment per machine as previously. Reduced production or an abnormally high wage were the result.

Regarding the introduction of new machines, one federation said that in some districts the unions had succeeded in retaining say three men on a particular piece of machinery which in other districts was handled successfully by one or two men.

Other restrictions mentioned were resistance to the installation of time clocks, to shift-working, or to systems of payment by results; the maintenance or extension of unreasonable wage differentials; insistence on unjustifiably large manning scales; and insistence on promotion by seniority.

Restrictions practised by workers but not attributed to unions included 'stint' working and other ways of limiting output, late starting and early finishing, unauthorized tea intervals, and going-slow when new plant was installed, with a view to the establishment of unduly high piece-rates.

Only five of the eleven federations were willing without qualification to have their information communicated to the N.J.A.C.

The National Joint Advisory Council decided that, while recognizing the difficulties of definition and identification, there was no doubt that there were in industry both practices and attitudes which could not in present circumstances be justified. There was some tendency, they said, to perpetuate practices because they had been reasonable enough in the circumstances prevailing at the time of their introduction or because they were embodied in agreements. The council felt strongly 'that such practices should be subjected to a new and searching examination to see whether, and to what extent, they still corresponded to the present needs of industry'.

The role of the council, they decided, was to stimulate and encourage industries to embark upon a joint examination of any problems they might have. With the support of the council, the Minister wrote to the British Employers' Confederation asking them to request employers' organizations in each industry to take the matter up with the unions and to report back, and wrote to the T.U.C. asking them to request the unions to cooperate. The confederation approached 190 employers' organizations covering the greater part of industry. In deference to the unions, the inquiry was described as dealing, not with restrictive practices, but 'practices impeding the full and efficient use of manpower'.

The response was very slow – one more indication of the inclination of employers in many industries to let sleeping dogs lie – and many reminders were necessary. The council did not think enough progress had been made to justify a report until January 1959, two and a half years after the inquiry began. They had then received replies from 112 of the 190 industries, but it was thought that they covered about seventy-five per cent of those in civilian employment. In addition to the industries which did not reply, large sections in national and local government, the health service, banking, insurance, and finance had not been covered by the inquiry.

Dividing the industries which did respond into three categories, the council found that sixty-four, covering twenty-nine per cent of the workers, reported they had no problem in regard to the efficient use of manpower. Another forty-two, representing thirty-nine per cent of the workers, had set up machinery to deal with any problems or appeared to be in process of doing so. The remaining six industries, representing seven per cent, needed more time or had been unable to undertake a joint examination.

'It is often said that industry is riddled with "restrictive practices" which no one on either side of industry has seen fit to tackle,' commented the council. 'It has been a source of satisfaction to learn that so many industries felt able to report that they were meeting no real difficulties in their efforts to ensure that manpower was efficiently used.'

Among the industries thus giving themselves a clean bill of health were atomic energy, boot and shoe manufacture, brass foundries, brewing, carpet manufacture, catering, cinemas, coal merchants, clothing, dyers and cleaners, farmers, food manufacture, glass containers, hairdressing, iron and steel scrap, laundering, leather goods manufacture, multiple shops, paper box manufacture, rubber manufacture, shipping, tin box manufacture.

The second category included some industries, like printing and port transport, which have been notorious for restrictive practices. It also included engineering, apparently because the industry has its procedural agreement for the settlement of disputes. A special statement signed by leaders of both sides in the engineering industry said that, while there might be room for improvement, they were not worse than anybody else and that great changes had taken place in the industry in the last half century with an almost incredibly small degree of friction.

The second category also included building, railways, chemicals, air transport, coal, cotton, electrical supply, furniture, hosiery, iron and steel, jute, foundries, retail meat, milling, pottery, vehicle building, and wool.

The six industries apparently getting nowhere were shipbuilding and repair, electrical contracting, private road haulage, heating, ventilating and domestic engineering, paper bag manufacture, and painting and decorating in Scotland.

The differences between the industries in the second and third categories were probably in many cases not very real. Whatever machinery the industries in the second category may have, it has certainly not always proved very effective, for widespread restrictive practices are known to have been in existence in some of them for many years and to continue.

Precise detail about these practices is hard to get, partly because of the reluctance of both sides to talk about them and partly because of the difficulty, for anyone not aware of all the circumstances, of deciding when a practice is restrictive. There is a special difficulty about printing, because of the reluctance of newspapers and other publications to print anything on the subject. They fear they may provoke bad feeling, and perhaps trouble, among their own employees, and they are aware of the difficulty of preserving impartiality on a subject with which they are directly concerned.

Yet the printing unions, by the strength of their closed shop policy, have established a stranglehold more complete than is to be found in any other industry. To all intents and purposes they have taken over control of labour, both in recruitment and in its day-to-day arrangements, except for technical matters.

The issue which has overshadowed others in this industry and has repeatedly been brought into the open has been the restriction on the number of apprentices, imposed in such a way that there has been a continuous shortage of craftsmen. Again and again employers have pleaded, cajoled, bargained, and threatened in the attempt to get more apprentices but they have never been more than partially successful.

Seldom has there been a dispute or inquiry in the industry in which this issue has not loomed over others. Throughout the prolonged dispute between the London Master Printers' Association and the London Society of Compositors, which led to an inquiry in 1950, the issues of wages and manpower ran side by side, and some other restrictive practices were brought in. At one stage, for instance, the union proposed that, in return for a minimum rate of £8, the ratio of apprentices to journeymen should be regulated by a sliding scale, under which the ratio would be fixed annually for the following twelve months in the light of the unemployment figures for the preceding twelve months.

Other matters raised were the possibility of extended overtime, permission for compositors' work done in the provinces to be printed in London, the introduction of incentive schemes, and 'dual working'. The last item referred to an agreement that a compositor cannot be transferred from one kind of work to another except by termination of his employment and by a fortnight's notice and re-engagement. Dual working would permit transfers between jobs without notice.

The employers complained to the court of inquiry that the union seemed bent on maintaining the serious shortage of compositors so that they could dictate their own terms to the industry. The union repeatedly emphasized their anxiety with regard to the possible recurrence of serious unemployment, and stressed their heavy obligations to their members in the shape of unemployment and superannuation benefits.

The court came to the conclusion that in their anxiety to avoid the risk of unemployment the union had sought to weight the scales in their own favour to an unreasonable extent, though they did not dispute that there was an acute shortage of labour in the industry. The court also thought the union was not justified in opposing the admission of adult entrants to be trained as compositors.

Six years later there was another dispute, this time involving the Association of Correctors of the Press as well as the London Typographical Society (as the L.S.C. had become) and another court of inquiry. The court found that in spite of agreement on a limited increase in the number of apprentices in 1950, there was still a manpower shortage and the employers – but not the union – still regarded it as acute.

Another practice which both courts commented upon was the insistence of the printing unions on separate negotiations. 'While the Joint Industrial Council provides machinery for the settlement of disputes, it has no authority to negotiate on wages,' commented the 1950 court. 'This limitation on the powers of the Council stems largely from the fear of the small craft unions that they would be out-voted by the much larger unions representing semi-skilled and unskilled workers. Uncoordinated claims must inevitably open the way to "leap-frogging" and militate against the formation of any balanced wage structure.'

The practice of the unions in this regard has varied. In 1959, nine of them negotiated together with the master printers and the Newspaper Society but each went its own way in negotiations with the Newspaper Proprietors' Association later in the year.

In 1959 we find priority once again being given to manpower in the negotiations which preceded the general printing and provincial newspaper strike. The first three of twenty-two points which the employers put to the unions concerned labour supply, and these were the only ones which they made a condition of their original offer of a forty-two-and-a-half hour week. They asked for apprentice intake ratios to be adjusted so that in firms of all sizes the proportion of apprentices to journeymen would be more nearly related to the labour requirements of the firm, a reduction in the period of apprenticeship in all crafts to five years, and for all unions to agree that no special procedure need be followed to indenture adult apprentices.

Some of the employers' demarcation proposals were summarized in Chapter 3. Others of their demands indicate the kinds of difficulties with which they were faced. They asked the unions to encourage the use of double day shifts, treble shifts, and night shifts, and for their cooperation in method study and work measurement incentive schemes. They also wanted new agreements about the use of justifying typewriters and photo composing and other new photographic techniques, and asked that the operation of new processes generally should be discussed jointly with all the unions affected, rather than with individual unions.

Efforts by employers to make the removal of restrictive practices a condition of wage settlements have often thrown light on practices of which the public would otherwise have heard nothing. Such efforts have been made in a number of industries, including coal mining, the railways, and shipbuilding. The unions call such conditions 'strings' and often oppose them, arguing that the right to a fair wage should not be subject to any conditions. Sometimes they have given vague undertakings that have usually had no practical result. Sometimes, in printing for instance, something has been achieved.

Moreover restrictions on the easy and free movement of labour from one job to another, and rigid traditions of the speed at which printing machines work and the time taken on a particular job, still hold back printing firms with more modern machines and up-to-date methods and prevent them from reducing prices.

The shipbuilding employers have repeatedly tried to make removal of restrictive practices a condition of wage settlements but so far with negligible results. As manpower restrictions are probably the most damaging practices in printing and absenteeism in mining, so demarcation is the most serious in shipbuilding. Something has been said of this in Chapter 3. Shipbuilding employers complain of many other restrictions, however. In their evidence to the court of inquiry into the 1957 wage dispute, they said that production was greatly impeded by absenteeism and loss of time during the working day and by strikes, without recourse to agreed procedure, and unofficial stoppages of work often accompanied by demands for more pay – particularly at crucial stages of the shipbuilding process. Other severe handicaps were embargoes on overtime, and 'ceilings' on earnings; restrictions on the recruitment of apprentices, especially in welding; refusal to accept work-study techniques and revision of obsolete piece-work prices; reluctance to use new machinery without double-manning, and refusal to accept a reasonable degree of interchangeability between trades.

The unions replied that they had to have regard to high standards of craftsmanship and they could not agree to practices which might result in skimped and inferior work; that the workers had in many cases made financial sacrifices to cooperate in the introduction of new machinery; that, in spite of the allegations made by the employers regarding absenteeism and such matters, the average hours worked in the industry were from forty-eight to fifty a week; that the wartime 'dilution' agreement was still in operation and gave the employers many facilities which were of great value to them. In many other respects, general and specific, the unions claimed to have cooperated with the employers to the employers' advantage.

A document prepared by the employers as a condition for a wage offer included undertakings by the unions to do their best to bring to an end without delay any stoppages of work, whether sectional or otherwise, embargoes on overtime in violation of the terms of an agreement, and restrictions on output or earnings. They were also asked to agree to use their full influence to facilitate the introduction of new techniques and their efficient operation, and to issue a statement to all their members drawing attention to the necessity of starting work promptly and of remaining at work until the recognized stopping times, and to the fact that men must not stop work during working hours for the purpose of attending union meetings without permission.

While no firm undertakings were given by the unions, it was agreed in the settlement of June 1957 that there would be joint meetings to discuss the issues raised. Two meetings were in fact held but achieved nothing.

In December 1957, Mr George G. Parker, president of the Shipbuilding Employers' Federation, wrote in *Lloyd's List Annual Review* that the increased output expected from heavy capital expenditure and new methods of construction had not materialized. A prerequisite to better results was that modern machines must be used to full capacity and not be overmanned. Another was the provision of an adequate labour force. A recent survey had shown that in three of the principal trades over 4000 more skilled men should be employed. A great deal of effort to attract new entrants was defeated by the insistence of certain trade unions on maintaining a fixed ratio of apprentices which bore no relation to the industry's needs.

The following February, in their reply to a union claim for a forty-hour week, the employers said they had not had the cooperation they were promised: 'Time lost by reason of late starting, early stopping, and absenteeism continues to be very considerable indeed. We are well aware that this is largely a matter for management, but it is equally a matter which could be vastly improved if we had your cooperation. So far, despite repeated requests, you have not seen fit to support us in efforts to ensure that men start work at the proper time and do not leave their work until the appropriate stopping time.

'Stoppages of work in the industry since last May number more than one thousand, and the total man-hours lost as a result of these stoppages has reached a figure of over half a million. Of this total, almost 400,000 man-hours were lost by the workers responsible for the stoppages and a further 110,000 by workers rendered idle as a direct result of such stoppages. Almost seventy-five per cent of these stoppages have been due to the holding of meetings which men have either left their work to attend, or which, having started during meal intervals, have extended into normal working hours. A very large percentage of these meetings have dealt with union matters and have not been concerned with working conditions or arrangements in the yards.' (Many of the stoppages mentioned would be too short to get into the Ministry of Labour Statistics.)

In 1958 the position seemed to be getting worse rather than better. Mr Parker calculated that there had been 1068 stoppages of work with a loss of 2,621,049 man-hours in the first nine months of that year. Nearly two mllion of the man-hours were lost as a result of two prolonged strikes of platers at Belfast and of drillers at Birkenhead, but the remaining 700,000 man-hours meant almost 80,000 a month. Mr Parker said that 226,500 man-hours were lost in 801 stoppages to hold meetings, 150,000 were lost as a result of 172 smaller strikes or mass absences from work (some of which coincided with mid-week football matches), and 228,000 were lost in 22 stoppages due to demarcation disputes. Some 7000 hours were lost in 72 stoppages from causes unknown to the managements.

A report of the Department of Scientific and Industrial Research at the end of 1960 said that the fullest use of shipyard space and capital equipment was handicapped by labour conditions and by the impracticability of shift working, which operates in a number of other countries.

The unions are never tired of pointing out that some shipyards produce output records and have few or no labour troubles. They conclude that where there is trouble, it is the fault of the management.

The same phenomenon is to be observed in other industries. On the docks, for instance, there has been a long period of cooperative work at Bristol and few difficulties at the south Wales ports, but in Liverpool and Birkenhead, in Glasgow, in London, and to a lesser degree in Hull, restrictive practices have caused much criticism.

A common complaint is that dockers do not do a full day's work. In London, Liverpool, and elsewhere it is said that excessive time is taken for morning and afternoon tea-breaks. Instead of some men going for tea while others continue, the work often stops completely. Organized 'spelling', which grew up during the war – a system by which members of a gang take it in turns to leave their work – is said to be still found in Glasgow and Liverpool. New mechanical devices are not directly opposed but there have been instances of the men insisting on such excessive manning scales as to prevent their introduction. There was a time, for instance, when fork-lift trucks were to be found lying idle in London and Liverpool, and certainly their general introduction was delayed by disagreements over the number of men who should man them.

Rules operated by the men sometimes result in a lack of mobility which wastes many hours. For instance, there was a continuity rule in London which said that when a gang had finished one hold of a ship, or a whole ship, they should return to the calling-on point, though several hours might be saved by transferring to another ship. Even more trouble was the zoning system in Glasgow, under which the dockers report at a particular calling-on point even though they know they will be working on a ship in a distant part of the port. Time is also wasted by the refusal of dockers to start work until a gang is made up, so that there may be long delays although there are enough men in several short-handed gangs to make up more than one full gang.

On the other hand absenteeism in the docks is negligible and demarcation disputes have been rare. It is said that the dockers generally work well but that there is a laxity in some ports which may be attributed to a large extent to the difficulties or inadequacies of supervision. Something has already been said of the readiness of dockers to strike on the slightest pretext.

The readiness of miners to strike on the slightest pretext is even more remarkable, though in their case it is largely limited to the three coalfields of Yorkshire, Scotland, and south Wales and the great majority of strikes are very short.

In the first decade after the war there was a continuous shortage of coal, and consequently a continuous drive to increase manpower and productivity. In this the union leaders cooperated to the best of their ability. They formed joint committees with the board to tour the coalfields. They agreed to setting up joint committees in the pits with power to fine persistent absentees. They agreed to Saturday working or an extra half-hour on the day after they had got the five-day week. They had their own recruitment officer. They agreed to foreign workers being brought in.

But in a number of ways they could not carry the working miners with them. The practice which above everything else held down improvements in output was absenteeism and every conceivable effort was made to reduce it, but in vain. There were temporary improvements at various times, but the men always went back to their old habits, and the position is now worse than ever.

Absenteeism in 1959 averaged 14·69 per cent – more than one man in seven off work all the time. And 8·74 per cent of it was classified as voluntary. The time lost through absenteeism is fifty times as much as the time lost through unofficial strikes.

It may also, perhaps, be accounted a restrictive practice that the men in many pits either delayed or prevented the employment of foreign workers when there was a desperate need of increased manpower – first Poles, then Italians, then Hungarians – but there were safety and social motives behind this, as well as restrictive ones.

Perhaps the other main complaint, apart from the propensity to strike, was that in some districts they often did not do a full day's work. They do their 'stint' and then clear out and there has always been strong resistance to increasing the 'stint'.

In building, as in shipbuilding, demarcation rules are one of the commonest limitations on output, but we have said enough about that in Chapter 4. Apart from this there are comparatively few restrictive practices in the industry, except for the laxity in discipline which is caused by shortage of labour and often results in such things as bad time-keeping and excessive tea-breaks. Restriction on entry into craft unions is not a problem.

One often hears talk of bricklayers limiting the number of bricks they lay in a day, but in the post-war years, when labour has been almost continuously short, complaints of that have been rare – except to spin out bricks when they are in short supply. That is not to say that output is at the maximum. Men employed by labour-only sub-contractors, whose very high wages depend on getting through a job in a very short time, may lay twice as many bricks in a day as a man on time rates.

The unions are strongly opposed to the system of labour-only sub-contracting, opposition which some employers regard as a restrictive practice in itself, but there are differences of view about that.

For a long time the unions resisted the introduction of bonus schemes, but that was overcome and now it is not uncommon to hear complaints from the men that not enough employers have adopted them.

Several of the most startling restrictions were found in the London markets, particularly Covent Garden and Smithfield. Some of the practices there resulted from the maintenance of wartime expedients no longer justified, and some arose during the adjustment to a free market after the removal of Government control.

At Covent Garden, if a consignment of fruit or vegetables was brought into the market area and dispatched to a customer without being handled at all, the pitchers still had to be paid as if they had unloaded it and the porters as if they had reloaded it. Retailers who collected their own produce had to pay a porterage fee as well. The pitchers, the staff men, and the porters had rigidly demarcated duties. Employers had to get their labour through the union markets officer, and had to take any worker they were given. The pitchers, who were self-employed, restricted their numbers to increase their earnings and this often resulted in long delays.

At Smithfield one complaint was that the drivers of the vehicles which take the meat away were no longer allowed to carry meat to their vehicles, so that they remained idle for hours at a time and there was more work for porters. Another rule forbade a driver or his mate to pull back the meat from the front of his vehicle to the tail-board, ready for the pitcher, with the result that there developed a new class of worker known as the puller-back.

Porters before the war used to wash their own trucks, but afterwards special men had to be employed for the job. There were detailed and time-wasting regulations about the time at which drivers might start and finish work. Retailers were not allowed to collect their own meat, but had to use 'bummaree' porters – as was mentioned in Chapter 5.

There was some case for some of these practices, but the position had clearly got out of hand. After long struggles at Covent Garden in 1957 and at Smithfield in 1958 the organization at both was improved so that some of the worst time-wasting practices were stopped.

Covent Garden is not the only place where men have to be paid on occasion for not working. An example of the same sort of thing is to be found in a film industry where the Association of Cinematograph and Television Technicians make strict conditions about the composition of a unit. A director may prefer to do some work himself, for instance the cutting of the film, but there will still have to be an editor on the pay-roll.

Official pressure to get rid of restrictive practices has been great ever since the war. The immense demand for goods and service in the immediate post-war period resulted in a continuing shortage of labour, and the Government was constantly urging on both sides of industry the need to make the fullest and most efficient use of limited manpower resources. Later on, the re-emergence of strong foreign competition in export markets impressed the need for the fullest efficiency upon employers.

Direct appeals to the unions were frequent. As early as March 1946, the T.U.C. called together the executive committees of all their affiliated organizations in London to a conference attended by the Prime Minister, Foreign Secretary, and Minister of Labour. A similar employers' conference took place the next day. The trade union delegates unanimously passed a resolution declaring their determination to do all in their power 'to accomplish the speedy reconstruction of industry to peace-time needs, to increase production and to utilize the nation's manpower, financial, and productive resources in order to ensure full employment and a steadily increasing supply of goods and services to meet the needs of the people and the demands of the export trade'. Regional conferences of unions and employers followed.

At the beginning of 1948, the T.U.C. issued a statement in which they said: 'It is no less a matter of direct self-interest than of social duty to assist by personal effort in obtaining the substantial and sustained increase in production which will alone enable the unions to defend the existing standards of life and to secure necessary improvements in the conditions of employment.'

In November the same year, there was another conference of executives to discuss how the level of productivity could be raised. A report prepared by the T.U.C. for the conference advocated numerous measures to increase productivity, including focusing attention on shortages and bottlenecks, organizing national or local industrial conferences, accelerating the formation of joint production committees, reviewing the system of shop stewards and other work-place representatives, and seeking to raise their efficiency, and education through colleges, union journals, and so on. They declared their intention of convening a series of conferences with unions to consider precise production problems in each industry.

Regarding restrictive practices specifically, they referred to the Pre-War Trade Practices Act, 1942, the application of which was still being postponed, and added: 'In so far as the problem exists, both sides of industry are involved. It is not one which can be satisfactorily dealt with in an atmosphere of recrimination: it requires careful examination by both union executives and management from the stand-point of its impact upon productivity.'

Following the conference of executives, the T.U.C. called meetings with groups of unions to discuss the subject, but the unions showed small interest and after a few months the campaign faded out. It did not appear to have made much impression.

The unions cooperated with the Government and the employers on the National Production Advisory Council on Industry, and on the regional boards, and district committees which dealt with numerous problems in the days of shortages of materials and manpower, and all the intricate adjustments that were needed to restore a peacetime economy.

In July 1948, they joined with the employers and their opposite numbers in the United States to form the Anglo-American Council on Productivity, which, in its four years of existence, sent nearly seventy joint productivity teams from British industries to America to study their methods of achieving high output. The teams' reports were circulated and reported on widely among British employers and workers.

When it came to an end in 1952, the British side set up the British Productivity Council, with the T.U.C. bearing its share of the cost. The purpose was 'to stimulate the improvement of productivity in every sector of the national economy by every possible means'. The council set up local productivity committees, of which there are now more than 100, in as many industrial communities as possible. Most unions were cooperative in most areas, though not all. Many of the local committees established circuit schemes, under which groups of firms exchanged visits of joint teams, and they have many other plans to increase interest in raising productivity. From the headquarters in London a work study unit visits all parts of the country and pamphlets, films, and other visual aids are distributed, and many other activities undertaken.

The T.U.C. also cooperated in the European Productivity Agency and for a period seconded to it their production officer, Mr E. Fletcher. The production department at the T.U.C. is a post-war addition to their services, set up in 1950.

They are represented on a number of other bodies concerned with productivity, such as the British Institute of Management, the British Standards Institution, and the Department of Scientific and Industrial Research. They are constantly pressing for union representation on the councils of industrial research associations, with some success. They call occasional one-day conferences on technical subjects and have included courses in production and management subjects at the trade union college. In 1959 they tried to persuade the Government and employers to make the N.P.A.C.I. a more effective body. They also, as was said earlier, cooperated in the N.J.A.C. inquiry into restrictive practices.

Altogether the T.U.C. have certainly not neglected these matters, but it can hardly be said that the undoubted enthusiasm at Congress House is reflected among all the union leaders, let alone among the men in the workshops. The changed attitude of mind, which could do far more than any direct attack to eliminate restrictive practices, is developing but slowly. Full employment has helped, probably more than propaganda, but old customs and traditions die hard.

9

LIGHT UNDER A BUSHEL

Distant Relations – Our Enemies, the Press – Untold Members

IT is a remarkable circumstance that neither of the two biggest
trade unions in the country, the Transport and General Workers'
Union and the Amalgamated Engineering Union, has anything
in the nature of a public relations department. The T.G.W.U. has
1,300,000 members. It is the dominating trade union power in
two important industries, road transport and the docks, and has
great influence in many others. Its funds amount to some
£10,800,000. The A.E.U. has a million members. It is by far the
biggest union in the biggest group of industries in the country
and has members in almost every industry. Its funds amount to
some £11,600,000. Yet neither has thought it worth while to employ skilled men to explain its actions and policy to the people or
to its own membership. Most smaller unions have been equally
unenterprising.

If it were not so, I might not now be writing this little book, for
no small part of the criticism which has been directed against the
unions in recent years has been the result of misunderstanding of
their policies and of the reasons for which they behave as they do.
The unions are by no means wholly to blame for that misunderstanding, but they are partly to blame. It is generally recognized
that in a modern democratic society the force of public opinion
is powerful. Governments fear it because they fear elections, but
election or no election they cannot go against it. The cold war
itself consists in great measure of a struggle for the support of
world opinion. Great nations protest and sulk if they are the
object of adverse criticism at the United Nations. All the devices
of modern publicity are used to explain and defend national
policies. Floods of radio propaganda cross and recross frontiers.
In thousands of newspapers, speeches, books, films, the battle is
unceasing.

At home every Government department has its public relations staff, describing, explaining, defending. Industrial firms and nationalized industries (with certain restrictions) are always at it. Millions have been spent by industry to influence public opinion against nationalization. The success or failure of their public relations policy means life or death to political parties. The only great national organizations which seem to think they need not bother about public relations are trade unions (and employers' bodies).

That last sentence is, of course, too sweeping. The T.U.C. has had a small publicity department for thirty years, and shared one with the Labour party before that. In recent years some trade unions (and employers' organizations) have made a beginning. The National Union of Railwaymen have a full-time publicity representative. The Union of Shop, Distributive and Allied Workers have had an active press and publicity department for twenty years. Several others have officers who combine other responsibilities, usually the editing of the union journal, with the job of press officer. Civil service and other white-collar unions, who are even more dependent on public opinion than those of manual workers because they cannot usually use the strike, devote more attention to public relations. The National and Local Government Officers' Association, to take one instance, have quite a strong department.

It is also true to say that many general secretaries and national officers are in a sense their own publicity officers. They often maintain friendly and helpful relations with the industrial and labour correspondents of newspapers, and are generally ready and even eager to appear on radio and television and to write (or sign) articles. And, of course, they issue statements and make speeches that are reported. Since Mr Frank Cousins became general secretary of the T.G.W.U. he has been constantly in the public eye and ear trying to explain his point of view.

But though many of these men have a natural instinct for publicity, they have had no training in the finer points of public relations and are often inadequate or clumsy. They seldom have any long-term public relations policy. Moreover, in the periods when it is most vital to make the maximum favourable impact on public opinion, during important negotiations and disputes, they are too busy to devote time and attention to it.

The contrast with American trade unions in this matter is striking. There the development of public relations has been a matter of self-defence, because of the great resources devoted by employers to publicity through radio and newspaper advertising, and other media. Most American unions have their own press or publicity departments and every local is expected to have its press and radio representative. Some have their own television programmes and stations. They issue pamphlets by the hundred thousand and make films and gramophone records. They work hard to establish mutual understanding with other sections of the community, such as farmers, professional men, clergy, and small business men. They circularize ministers of religion and school teachers. They encourage their members to play an active part in the life of every locality, with committees to promote such participation and collections of large sums for social objects. In 1956 the A.F.L.–C.I.O. issued a ten-point statement of policy on community action. The first two points were:

'The union member is first and foremost a citizen of his community.

'The union member has a responsibility to his community. He must cooperate with his fellow citizens in making his community a good place in which to live, to work, to raise children. He must be concerned about the availability of adequate health, welfare, and recreational services for the whole community.'

The unions compete with employers in trying to get their point of view presented in the schools.

When an important new contract is under negotiation, or a strike is taking place, or a recruiting drive is under way, large sums are spent on radio and television and press advertising. The struggles with employers are to a large extent struggles for the support of public opinion, with every device of modern public relations brought into use. Even in industries where relations are good it is recognized by both sides that membership and public have an interest in knowing what is going on.

A remarkable example of this is the system of 'fishbowl' negotiations adopted in the West Coast paper industry, a syste---

167

which allows representatives of management and workers from every mill to be present during negotiations and listen to what is going on, so that they can spread an understanding of all the considerations that have given rise to the final agreement.

There are, of course, disadvantages as well as advantages in such semi-public negotiations. In some industries in this country, of which steel is an outstanding example, negotiations are often carried through and concluded without anybody outside knowing anything about it. Both sides take the view that it is easier to reach agreement if they are not hampered by a general knowledge of what they have said at every stage; especially because it is hard to withdraw from a position taken in public. There is something to be said for it, but it is hardly possible except where there is a very close understanding between employers and unions – and where wages and conditions are so good that union members are rarely dissatisfied. In such circumstances, the only party likely to have a complaint is the general public.

In most industries there is usually a struggle, and there is no doubt that public opinion plays a big part in determining the final result. That is perhaps particularly true of strikes, but it is often important during the normal negotiating procedure. In these circumstances the neglect of public relations by the unions – and employers – is hard to understand. Union members often seem to feel that everything would come all right if only everybody understood their plight, as is shown by the frequent demands by engineering unions and others for 'national campaigns' to put their case across. Yet conference resolutions asking for the establishment of public relations or press departments are more often than not defeated. They cost money.

The reasons for this muddled attitude are complex. Partly it is a sort of race memory of the days when unions were illegal and every activity had to be conducted in secret. Allied to that, perhaps going deeper, is the belief, based on generations of experience, that every man's hand is against them. They take a bitter pride in their isolation. They believe that anything they do or say will be distorted. So they must face the inevitable unpopularity and obloquy and rely on their own strength and solidarity, defying the capitalists, the Government, the law, the establishment, and the press.

Suspicion of the press is ingrained and not unjustified. There are papers which will seize on anything discreditable to the unions and magnify it out of all proportion to its news value. Some will misrepresent the union attitude and one or two, particularly during disputes, indulge in scurrilous personal attacks which do not spare a union leader's home or family. They do not treat employers in the same way. On the other hand, there are papers which attempt to give fair treatment to both sides and to explain their points of view in so far as they are made understandable, and certain of these papers are leaders of opinion. And, of course, there are one or two papers which take the union side, right or wrong, and frequently misrepresent the employers.

The weight of numbers is against the unions, but it remains true that if they explain their case clearly their explanation will be published in most papers, at least in part, and they will on the whole get much better treatment than if they don't. The American unions, certainly with no less hostile a press, have found that to be so. So have those unions in this country which have made the experiment, of which the most notable example is the National Union of Railwaymen. Their executive, after one dispute, passed a unanimous resolution thanking the press for their attitude throughout. That could never have happened if they themselves had not had a helpful publicity department. A skilled adviser can often save trade union leaders from laying themselves open to the kind of attack of which they complain.

The behaviour of inexperienced, unofficial strike committees is illuminating. When the dispute begins, they are usually antagonistic to the press and will often say nothing to them or confine their information to inadequate and clumsily expressed official statements or resolutions. But by the end of the dispute, if it lasts any length of time, they will have appointed a press officer, started calling press conferences, sought out correspondents, and may be getting a better show for their point of view than is given to the attitude of the employers or to the official union policy, if the union is one of those that do not trouble about public opinion.

The union attitude to radio and television differs somewhat from their attitude to the press. In general they consider these media also to be antagonistic, but when the actual words of a trade union leader are heard, it is impossible to complain of misrepresentation. Moreover most union leaders, while they like to see their names in print, like even more to see their own faces on the screen.

There are other reasons why unions dispense with public relations or press departments. One is simply money. The salaries of the officers in many unions are so low that they would have to pay more to get a competent public relations or press officer than they give their general secretary or full-time president. The salary scale would be thrown completely out of joint. That is one of the most important considerations with the A.E.U.

Another reason is the reluctance of general secretaries to entrust to anyone else the responsibility of speaking on behalf of the union. This is an important factor in the T.G.W.U. Reluctance to delegate authority is a characteristic weakness of trade union leaders, but in this case the attitude, widespread though it be, is based on a misunderstanding of the functions of public relations and press officers.

Yet another reason against giving timely information to press and radio is that it is contrary to union etiquette. Members must be told about it before anyone else. Otherwise they will complain: 'The first we heard of it was when we read it in the papers.' There is in fact something more than etiquette in this. There are times when a decision requires more careful explanation than most newspapers will have the space or perhaps the will to provide. It is not usually a question of explaining to the rank and file, who won't know anything about it except what they read in the newspapers anyway, but of explaining to local officials and delegates. But it is not easy to keep an important decision secret, and there is always the risk that it will get out in a garbled form that will do more damage than 'telling the papers first'. Experience has shown that union leaders badly need expert advice and help on such occasions.

Apart from decisions on special occasions, there seems no reason why the union attitude should not be explained publicly as soon as possible. An important reason for doing this is that, as has just been remarked, the only knowledge most members have of the national activities of their union is what they see in the newspapers. Which brings us to the vitally important question of relations between leaders and members or, as the modern jargon has it, 'internal communications'.

One of the most important causes of unrest in the unions is the ignorance of the general membership about what their leaders are doing and the reasons why they are doing it (or not doing it). Delay and inaction are often reasonable and justifiable, but they need to be explained. Members in the dark are easily misled by unofficial leaders.

Often enough wildcat strikers, encouraged by shop stewards or other unofficial leaders, will refuse even to listen to a union official. They have been fed with misrepresentations and to allow them to hear a fair account of the situation would endanger the strike. It has happened often on the docks, and in numerous other industries.

An incident in the 1958 B.O.A.C. dispute illustrates the power of shop stewards to stand in the way of communications between union leaders and members. The chairman of the trade union side of the national sectional panel advised the shop stewards that they should recommend members to lift the ban on overtime. The shop stewards had a meeting and decided that the ban should go on, so the members never received the official advice.

Trouble-makers often take advantage of inadequate communications, but trouble may arise without their aid. The British Oxygen strike in 1959, for instance, seems to have been caused mainly by what seemed to the workers inordinate delay in negotiations for higher wages. Some of the branches had begun to ask the unions for a new wage claim a year earlier, in October 1958. The leaders did not think they could justify a wage claim at that time and in April 1959, they put in for a forty-hour week and three weeks holiday; after some negotiations they got the three weeks holiday for those with fifteen years service. They did not give notice to the employers of an intended wage claim until July 1959.

The rank and file seemed to be unaware of all this. All they knew was that they had asked for an increase and after a year their leaders were still talking. So they started their strike – a strike which could almost certainly have been avoided if the general workers' unions had been more adept in keeping their members informed.

A *News Chronicle* Gallup Poll in 1954 suggested that forty per cent of trade unionists did not know the name of their general secretary and twenty-five per cent did not know the name of their branch secretary. In the 1959 trade union Gallup Poll, sixteen per cent of trade unionists and thirty-two per cent of all those questioned could not name any prominent trade union leader. Only forty-six per cent of unionists said they had been to a branch meeting within the past twelve months and thirty-two per cent never went.

Yet obviously they valued their trade union membership. Ninety per cent thought they had benefited from being a member of a union. Only seven per cent had first joined a union unwillingly. Sixty-five per cent thought that trade unions were efficient and only eleven per cent that they were not.

Rather unexpectedly, seventeen per cent said their sympathies had been with the employers in the pay disputes of the year and only a little more than half said their sympathies had been with the workers.

Comprehensive information about the level of branch attendances is difficult to get at, but Mr B. C. Roberts, of the London School of Economics, made a careful analysis of available information about the largest unions in *Trade Union Government and Administration in Great Britain*, published in 1956. While there was a good deal of variation, he found that average attendances seemed to range from three to fifteen per cent and that in most unions the average was from four to seven per cent. The

Amalgamated Society of Woodworkers seemed to have an average of about fifteen per cent, and figures for other craft unions were relatively high, but at meetings of miners' lodges (in Yorkshire, Durham, and south Wales) attendances averaged two or three per cent. Attendances at branches of general unions were usually below five per cent and sometimes below one per cent. Generally the bigger the branch the smaller the proportion attending.

In *Government of British Trade Unions* (1952), Dr Joseph Goldstein, an American research student, described a branch of the Transport and General Workers' Union, with more than 1000 members, run by twenty-five or thirty active members who conducted the business, divided the offices between them, and even filled in the members' voting papers. Within the twenty-five or thirty was an inner circle of six or seven who decided the branch's policy. Part of the time they were nearly all Communists, but when they all left the party together, procedure continued as before. He interviewed a number of the inactive members of the branch and found that nearly eight out of every ten had never read the union journal, and half of those had never heard of it.

Dr Goldstein also asked them why they did not attend branch meetings. They mentioned such things as a sense of feeling out of place at branch meetings, inconvenience of time and place, domestic duties, general indifference, and dissatisfaction with the operation of the branch. Many single women thought the meetings were primarily for men.

Two out of every ten members, mostly older ones, said they were too tired to go to meetings in the evening. About a third mentioned household duties and family responsibilities, especially married men under forty and almost all the married women. A few married men were not allowed to go to meetings by their wives and many liked to spend their leisure time with their children. Many preferred to spend their time on such things as painting and decorating, building repairs, poultry and rabbit keeping, gardening, and even shoe-repairing.

A quarter of the women and a tenth of the men said they were unaware of the existence of regular branch meetings. Some just said they were not interested. They paid their subscriptions and the rest was up to the union. After they left work they wanted to forget about the factory.

Since Dr Goldstein conducted his inquiries, television has become a major competitor of the branch meeting.

Mr Roberts also analysed a number of ballot votes for union officers. Among unions in which members can only vote at branch meetings, the average poll for senior national officers was nearly sixteen per cent in the Amalgamated Society of Woodworkers and just under ten per cent in the Amalgamated Engineering Union. In the National Union of Boot and Shoe Operatives, where additional polling places are provided, the average was rather more than 11·4 per cent. In the Electrical Trades Union and the Amalgamated Union of Building Trade Workers, whose ballot papers are distributed by branch secretaries and may be returned to him in various ways, the percentage returns were mostly between twenty and thirty. In the Transport and General Workers' Union, where only the general secretary is elected, voting has been as high as fifty per cent. Nearly seventy per cent voted in elections for members of the executive council of the British Iron, Steel and Kindred Trades Association and from sixty-five to seventy-five per cent in votes for national officers of the National Union of Mineworkers. The miners vote at the pit-head as they go to or leave work.

The general conclusion appears to be that the more voting is limited to branch meetings, the fewer take part, and the closer it comes to the place of work, the more take part. It is also no doubt true that there is more interest in unions which only elect one or two chief officers when the old ones retire, like the T.G.W.U. and the N.U.M. than in unions in which every officer comes up for re-election every few years, so that contests are going on all the time, like the A.E.U. and the E.T.U.

Union membership is a part of the working side of a man's life and participation in union activities depends on relating them as closely as possible to his work.

The Gallup Poll quoted above asked trade unionists where they got information about the affairs of their union. Of one hundred and forty replies, thirty-five said from shop stewards, thirty-four the notice board at work, and twenty-seven talk at work. Only eighteen mentioned the union journal and seventeen circulars. Five mentioned other ways and four said they did not bother. It is said to be not uncommon for workers to be unaware of the rights to benefits and assistance which membership of their union may give them.

The means of internal communication at the disposal of the leadership include letters and circulars, visits to branches, the union journal, educational courses, and the holding of conferences. By none of these do they normally reach more than a small proportion of their members, the majority of whom take little interest except in times of dispute.

Because of the small attendance, branch letters and circulars, or an official speaking at a branch meeting, are not themselves any answer to the problem, though they are of great importance because they do reach the active core. It is essential, therefore, that the written matter should be clear and comprehensive without being so tedious as to drive members away from meetings. This is something which many unions could well study much more carefully than they have done. Apart from statements which have been written or edited by one of the few journalists on its staff, the T.U.C. does not set a good example in the use of clear and simple English, as some of the quotations in this book have illustrated. Trade unionism has developed its own jargon.

Visits by union officers as frequently as possible can help the active members better than any circular to understand what is going on, and can also do much to prevent the sense of neglect and isolation suffered by many branches in big unions. In some unions national officers tour the country regularly at week-ends to visit districts and branches. Others do so when some important development in policy requires explanation. But in some unions national officers are permitted to visit branches only if invited. Officers of the National Union of Seamen regularly visit ships in port at home and abroad, but supporters of the unofficial movement in 1960 complained of lack of contact with the union.

Union practice and efficiency varies a great deal. Many badly need their administration brought up to date. Some send out circulars every few days, some every few months. Some, but not all, make it a rule that they must be read aloud. The full minutes of executive meetings are circulated in some unions, while in others there are only short records of agreements or administrative decisions. Branches usually meet once a fortnight or once a month, sometimes less frequently. Many unions send to branches leaflets, posters, and recruiting propaganda for distribution.

It is assumed that shop stewards will attend branch meetings and spread around news of what the union is doing, but there is no reason to suppose that they do so very effectively. Sometimes they misrepresent what the union is doing. Some unions provide for members' meetings called by stewards at their place of work, but they are an exception. A disadvantage of this method of disseminating information is that members will more than ever regard it as unnecessary to attend branch meetings.

Some unions have realized the need to simplify and clarify circulars and other union documents, to reduce the volume of business at branch meetings, and to develop education courses which include training for shop stewards and branch officials in giving concise reports, but many others have made little or no effort in this direction. There is certainly a long way still to go. Many officials are content to say that if a member wants to know what is going on, he should attend his branch meeting – and leave it at that.

The T.U.C. publishes a monthly magazine, *Labour*, with a circulation of some 15,000, and the fortnightly duplicated *Industrial News*, mainly for the assistance of the editors of union journals. There are about ninety national trade union journals of some sort, and some local ones as well. They may have a total circulation in the neighbourhood of 1,500,000, but their readership is probably much smaller. There is one weekly – the *Railway Review* – which was founded in 1880 and probably sells between 20,000 and 30,000 copies at 3*d*. each. *New Dawn*, the journal of the Union of Shop, Distributive and Allied Workers, is also sold and has a similar circulation. Of the biggest unions, the National

Union of Mineworkers alone has no journal – merely a factual bulletin. Some areas of the union have their own publications.

The journals vary greatly in style and quality. Most are in magazine form and are free to members. The *Railway Review* is a lively weekly newspaper combining vigorous comment with much information about the activities of the various sections of the union and the latest news of national negotiations. *Public Service*, the publication of the National and Local Government Officers' Association, had to appear in newspaper form during the printing strike of 1959, and it was decided to keep it that way. Early in 1960 the Amalgamated Union of Building Trade Workers replaced their magazine (circulation 14,500) with an eight-page newspaper, *Builders' Standard*, of which they hoped to distribute 70,000 copies.

A few of the periodicals can rival commercially published magazines in appearance, but many are slipshod, dull, and un-informative, produced by a general secretary or other official in odd moments, with little money at his disposal and less journa-listic experience, relying, apart from an article by the editor, largely on 'hand-outs' from the T.U.C., Labour party, and other organizations, and 'fill-ups' from the *Daily Herald*.

Others contain scarcely broken masses of district reports, financial statements, lists of names and addresses, and circulars. Few have much to say about current negotiations.

The journals would seem to present an admirable opportunity for the rank and file to make their views heard in letters to the editor. Some, like the *Railway Review*, *Red Tape*, the journal of the Civil Service Clerical Association, and *The Draughtsman*, the journal of the Association of Engineering and Shipbuilding Draughtsmen, take full advantage of it. But the majority, aston-ishingly, do not publish letters at all.

An article a few years ago in *The Post*, one of the better union publications, suggested that the objectives of a trade union journal should be 'to inform, to educate, to enthuse, to publicize'. For only a handful could it be claimed that those objectives are being achieved. It is probable that the news sheets published by shop stewards' committees are more read by the workers in the factories than the official union journal. Certainly the official journals can only reach a small proportion of the membership. The T.G.W.U. *Record* has a circulation of some 200,000 for 1,300,000 members, the A.E.U. *Journal* of about 150,000 for nearly a million.

From a long-term point of view the delegate conference is in many ways the most important point of contact between the leadership and the active members. The annual (or biennial or triennial) conferences vary in size from that of the National Union of Teachers, with 2300 delegates, to the meetings of the national committee of the Amalgamated Engineering Union, with fifty-two. They vary in length from a day to a fortnight – or even longer when unions are considering revisions to rules – but one week is most usual.

These are in theory the policy-making bodies of the union, but, in the case of the larger conferences at least, their more important function is to act as a sounding board of rank-and-file opinion and an opportunity for the leaders to explain and defend their conduct of affairs during the past year and their plans for the future. The size of some modern unions presents a problem, unknown when conferences began, in that if every branch is to be represented, the assembly becomes unwieldy, as have those of the teachers, the National and Local Government Officers' Association, and the Union of Shop, Distributive and Allied Workers. On the other hand the indirect selection of delegates from areas or districts, to which others of the largest unions have resorted, reduces the value of the conference in giving the branches a sense of playing an effective part in the conduct of affairs.

Very small conferences, like that of the A.E.U., have not the advantage of being representative and easily come under the influence of an organized clique.

Some unions, like the N.U.R. and U.S.D.A.W., have a series of conferences for different sections of their members. The annual conference of the post-office workers splits into three sections for part of the time. The A.E.U. have special conferences for women and youths. The Electrical Trades Union hold a youth conference. The Iron and Steel Trades Confederation, who have no national conference, have a series of district conferences. Some unions have district conferences as well as national conferences. The National Union of Agricultural Workers have county conferences during the winter. The Confederation of Shipbuilding and Engineering Unions and some individual unions call regular shop stewards' conferences. There are also, as has been mentioned in Chapter 5, unofficial shop stewards' conferences in a number of industries.

Special delegate conferences are also used by some unions to consult the membership on important policy decisions or proposals for new agreements. The miners and the busmen do this regularly. Ballots of membership are often taken by some unions, for instance in printing, before a strike is called, and by the miners on other policy decisions.

Large executives of lay members, which are quite common, fulfil something of the same functions as a conference, on a smaller scale but more continuously.

Delegate conferences are not only important as a means of communication from the leaders to the membership, but even more for communications upwards. Members can also make their views known to the leaders by sending up resolutions from the branches, though they may have to be filtered through the districts, by sending up their minutes (compulsory in some cases), by writing letters to headquarters or to the journal (if it publishes letters), by voting for officers, by leaving the union, or for that matter by unofficial strikes.

Apart from the last, unsatisfactory, ways of expressing their views, the various devices, if properly used, can form a satisfactory link between the leadership and the active members, but leave the bulk of the indifferent mass almost completely untouched. There is no known trade union channel which can reach the majority of them, but they can be reached by means of newspapers, radio, and television.

The unions are beginning to awaken to the possibilities, at least as a supplement to pamphlets and the direct approach, of other media for the purpose of reaching non-unionists during recruiting drives. The T.G.W.U. has experimented with film strips. The National Union of Tailors and Garment Workers produced a gramophone record in 1961. Both the National Union of General and Municipal Workers and the Electrical Trades Union spent small sums on television advertising in 1959 and in 1960 the A.E.U. decided to buy advertisement space on London tube trains. The use of such expensive media must be limited, however, so long as contributions remain at such a low level.

10

WHAT ABOUT THE BOSS?

Guilty Silence – Divisions at the Top – Knuckling Under to the Stewards –
Priority for Prerogatives – Chances Missed

PERHAPS one day someone will write a Penguin Special called
'What's Wrong with the Employers' Organizations?' There must
be ample scope, but very few people are qualified to do it. I barely
know enough about them – enough that is interesting – to fill this
short chapter.

They grew, and have their being, in a decent obscurity. If the
trade unions hide their light under a bushel, the employers'
organizations hide theirs under a haystack. No journalist waits
on the doorstep and no statements are issued after the meetings
of the council of the British Employers' Confederation, as happens after the meetings of the T.U.C. General Council. While 300
journalists and broadcasting representatives attend the annual
Trades Union Congress, the annual general meeting of the B.E.C.
is held in private, with a short official statement issued after-
ward.

They have a special committee on wages and conditions, which
the T.U.C. has not, where they exchange views on the current
wages situation. The discussions of this committee are obviously
of the utmost importance in relation to the current round of wage
negotiations, but nothing is ever heard of them. There are no
'leaks' to the Press.

Occasionally, when a wage claim is under discussion, some
attention is paid to meetings of the management board of the
Engineering and Allied Employers' National Federation, the
most important organization affiliated to the B.E.C., but otherwise employers' meetings pass unnoticed.

The B.E.C. issued no public statement on any general question
between 1931 and 1955. Since then they have become slightly
more articulate. They still have no public relations department,

but they now have an officer who receives Press inquiries. And their fortnightly bulletin and annual report, which used to be top secret documents, are now sent to the press.

Sometimes they display jealousy of the attention given to the T.U.C., but they remain fearful of publicity. The confederation has even less authority over its members than has the T.U.C. General Council and is always anxious lest it should give offence to some of them by a publicly expressed opinion. To disclose any difference of opinion within their ranks would be regarded as frightful.

The propaganda from the other side about the wickedness of employers has gone on so long that they suffer from a sense of guilt even now that public sympathy has turned against the unions. They themselves sometimes seem to be ashamed of being employers and having an employer's point of view. They have begun to realize the part that public opinion plays in industrial settlements, but they have yet to draw the obvious conclusions.

At a British Employers' Confederation conference in 1955 it was lamented that trade unions got more Press notice than did employers in disputes, partly because they were more ready to make their views known, and it was asserted that employers could not afford to be 'remote and secretive'. Employers seem to have taken even less notice than unions usually do of T.U.C. statements.

Some employers' organizations, for instance those in engineering and shipbuilding and building, have appointed public relations or press officers in recent years. The Building Employers' Federation in particular have realized the importance of publicity not only in their dealings with the outside world but also in their dealings with their own members. But the majority have no conception of modern public relations methods. Curiously enough, two of the most backward are the Newspaper Proprietors' Association and the Newspaper Society.

Of course newspapers do not treat employers' leaders in the way they treat union leaders. The yellow press do not describe their odd behaviour in their homes, or interview their children on their way from school, or take photographs of them with glasses of drink in their hands, or itemize the meals they eat in four-star hotels and quote the prices. Newspapers, after all, are run by employers.

The 'splits' and 'rows' that are constantly discovered in the trade union movement are seldom found among the employers, though of course they exist, as they do in all organizations. During the ten years or so after the war, when the B.E.C. and the Federation of British Industries were vainly trying to amalgamate, relations were constantly strained. One source of contention was the fact that the B.E.C. were tenants of the F.B.I. They were made to feel like poor relations (their income is much smaller than that of the F.B.I.) and they resented it. Personal antipathies were always on the boil. Since they moved to their own offices and gave up the attempt at amalgamation, relations have much improved and their leaders now meet regularly.

The permanent split in the employers' ranks remains in some respects a disadvantage, however. The B.E.C. is the only central organization representing employers as employers, but even in that capacity they are only partially representative because they exclude the nationalized industries. Both the nationalized industries and the B.E.C. are represented on the Minister of Labour's National Joint Advisory Council.

The division of employers' representation on trade matters is much more serious. No fewer than four national bodies, the B.E.C., the F.B.I., the National Union of Manufacturers, and the Association of Chambers of Commerce, each representing different points of view, have to be represented on the Chancellor of the Exchequer's National Production Advisory Council on Industry, not to mention the nationalized industries. And in addition to all these is the Institute of Directors, often talking with quite a different voice. In striking contrast is the position of the T.U.C., speaking on all matters on behalf of all major groups of employees except the teachers and the local government officers.

Within particular industries, internal communications are more rudimentary than those of unions. Divisions between employers seem to be just as great as between unions and sometimes result in actual splits. Soon after the war, for instance, Standard Motors broke with the engineering employers – they have since rejoined – and more recently the Steel Company of Wales broke away from the Steel Federation. For several years engineering employers have been in conflict about plans for a new wage structure for the industry. Important splits in the Confederation of Shipbuilding and Engineering Unions or the Iron and Steel Trades Confederation would make headline news, but among employers they escape notice except perhaps for a passing reference in the *Financial Times* or *The Times*. Some big firms, for instance Ford and Vauxhall in engineering, are permanently outside their federation.

Divisions between big firms and the medium-sized and small ones, as represented by the F.B.I. and the N.U.M. respectively, are also commonly found within individual employers' organizations. A few years ago, Lord Chandos and a number of other big industrialists lost patience with the negative attitude of the Engineering Federation. They expressed their views privately and formally but with great clarity. As a result the federation appointed ten vice-presidents, including a number of the critics. The critics regarded this as a palace revolution but the others regarded it as a method of silencing them. It has certainly had no noticeable effect on the policy of the federation.

Restiveness is sometimes to be found, too, among employers' groups outside London. There has been talk among some Midlands engineering leaders about the possibility of breaking away from the National Federation, though it has never come to anything.

If one looks through the criticism made of trade unions, one finds that nearly always there are comparable criticisms which can be made of employers. The leadership is often inadequate, partly because many of the big men will not spare the time to take part in the deliberations of the employers' organizations. Many employers indeed, in origin lawyers or accountants or production experts, have little knowledge of labour relations and under-rate their importance.

They have not, any more than the trade unions, found any solution to the problem of wages policy in times of full employment nor made much attempt to do so. The B.E.C. is content to assert from time to time that wage increases or reductions in hours are against the national interest, and the only constructive suggestion to come from it is that workers should be educated in the economic arguments which suggest that conclusion.

The attitude of most employers' organizations is merely to say 'no' to every claim until they are subjected to sufficient pressure to induce them to make a concession, but even then they stretch out the negotiations as long as possible. Meanwhile, when manpower is limited, their members engage in unrestricted competition for labour, offering bonuses and fringe benefits and overtime as inducements, so that they cannot be said to be raising standard rates.

Discipline is certainly no more effective than it is in the unions. Building employers in many parts of the country have regularly advertised for craftsmen at twice the standard rate or more. Many engineering firms, bus operators, and others will tell you that they can only get labour by promising regular overtime whether it is required or not.

In a statement on *Britain's Industrial Future* in 1955, the British Employers' Confederation ventured a timid remonstrance: 'In conditions of shortage of particular classes of labour, individual employers may seek to attract essential workers by offering superior wages and working conditions. It is natural that individual workers should take advantage of this situation. Where such employers and workers are members of employers' organizations and trade unions which have negotiated collective agreements on their behalf, they are, however, under a moral obligation not to subvert those agreements by extravagant bidding up in this way. Incentive schemes, moreover, must be devised so as to provide real incentives to effort; otherwise they may be merely a disguised method in present conditions of attracting labour from one employer to another. On a larger scale, employers' organizations and trade unions must themselves avoid engaging in a competitive race between industries which would frustrate any attempt to halt inflation.'

On rare occasions, an industrialist makes a constructive suggestion. In 1957, for instance, Lord Chandos, speaking as president of the Institute of Directors, proposed that, over the greater part of British industry, there should be automatic annual wage increases of perhaps $2\frac{1}{2}$ per cent for five years, with no new wage claims during the period. The object was to avoid the disturbance caused by the annual wage struggle. The trade unions did not appear hostile to the principle behind the idea. Lord Swinton drew attention to it in the House of Lords. But that was the end of it. Neither the engineering employers nor any other employers' organization made any comment.

The structure of the employers' organizations is in some ways as confused as that of the unions. The division of function between the B.E.C. and the F.B.I. is reflected in many industries, in which trade associations deal with trade matters and employers federations with labour relations. There may not be so much overlapping within industries as in the unions but, as has been pointed out, there is nothing in the trade union movement comparable to the competing national employers' organizations. If the division of the railway unions results in leap-frogging wage claims, so does the division of the bus employers between London Transport, the municipal employers, and the private employers.

The power of a union with a closed shop to take away a man's livelihood was paralleled by the employers' secret courts which could throw a tradesman out of business, and employers' associations have been riddled with restrictive practices, as is indicated by the number and variety of trade agreements registered under the Restrictive Trade Practices Act. This is not the place to go into these things. Legal action has been taken against these abuses, and that has contributed to the demand for legal action against trade union abuses.

But not all employers' restrictions can be dealt with under the Act. The unions in the printing industry, and some of those in shipbuilding, are criticized for unreasonably limiting the number of apprentices, but the chief cause of the shortage of apprenticeships in most industries is that the employers do not provide sufficient opportunities for training. Some firms, particularly the smaller ones, instead of training their own craftsmen, rely on those trained elsewhere. One would have supposed that any forward-looking industry would ensure there were adequate training facilities to provide the craftsmen they will need in the future, but they do not.

Employers are parties, too, to many agreements which authorize labour practices generally regarded as restrictive, and in many cases have made little effort to revise them. Their reluctance to raise such issues, unless compelled to do so by competition, has contributed to their perpetuation.

Moreover the weakness and short-sightedness of many employers have contributed to the power of unofficial leaders in the trade union movement. Time and again they have refused concessions when approached in a constitutional way by union representatives, but have given way almost immediately in face of an unofficial strike or the threat of it. Naturally this has strengthened the position of the unofficial leaders and given the workers the impression that wild-cat strikes are the best way to obtain reults.

Some employers are well aware of this. Sir Halford Reddish, chairman and managing director of a cement company, said in a speech in London in February 1960 that in his view employers must take the larger share of the blame for wildcat strikes.

'We must all admit that the weakness of so many employers, in private industry and in nationalized industries alike, toward flagrant breaches of contract is an important factor. . . .

'A man honours his bargain with his employer and does not come out on an unofficial strike; a man honours his implied bargain by doing his best in return for his wages, by working well but perhaps too well for the liking of some subversive shop steward. And what happens?

'All too often the employer meekly gives in, sacks a man, throws a human soul on to the scrap heap because he hasn't got the guts to stand up to the threat of the unofficial strike – engineered by the scheming few, acquiesced in by the unthinking many.

'After all, the man who gives in to a threat loses his self respect. But he also stores up more trouble, not only for himself but also for others. The blackmailer always comes back. The one who doesn't has yet to be born. Once breach of contract is seen to pay – in the purely material sense – then you can be sure it will be repeated.'

The B.E.C. referred to the subject in their bulletin in October 1959: 'A fairly common complaint by responsible trade union leaders is not that employers are too tough in their relations with their workpeople but that they are sometimes too weak. Examples showing that there is some justice in this complaint in industries under both public and private control will occur to everyone. Local pressure has often been allowed to interfere with agreed plans to close an uneconomic pit, to introduce a new machine to perform a loading or unloading task at a dock, or even to transfer a single man to a new job.'

They concluded that employers guilty of such weakness 'do a disservice not only to themselves but to all engaged in industry, including those officials of trade unions who are seeking to maintain relations on a sound and businesslike basis'.

As has already been remarked, there are many employers who have never understood or thought it worthwhile attempting to understand labour relations, and sometimes their clumsiness is unbelievable. Occasionally they have seemed to be deliberately provocative.

One of the most remarkable examples of that was in 1959 when the engineering employers issued a booklet in which they declared that in both 1954 and 1957 they were prepared to 'fight it out' with the unions, and blamed the Government for appeasement because they set up courts of inquiry instead of allowing them to do so. The unions' capacity to pay strike benefit, they pointed out, was limited. Naturally enough, the unions leaders regarded this as provocative and it has been constantly quoted since. The damaging effect of such a statement on relations in the industry is likely to last a long time.

The British Motor Corporation, when in 1956 they dismissed 6,000 men at forty-eight hours' notice without prior consultation, were inviting the bitterness and conflict with which the firm's operations have been hampered ever since. In March 1960, Mulliner's Tile Hill factory, making car bodies for the Standard company, suddenly closed down, giving its 150 employees a week's pay in lieu of notice.

The contrast between the experiences of different concerns in the same industry implies that there must be, or have been, grave faults in management in some of them. How else account for the constant trouble at the British Motor Corporation and Ford's and the relative freedom from trouble at Vauxhall's and Rootes? How else account for the frequency of disputes at two shipyards and their rarity in many others? How else explain that there are so many more strikes in the coalfields of Yorkshire, Scotland, and south Wales than in the others?

Sir Thomas Williamson, a union leader of unquestioned responsibility, said in an interview in the *Daily Telegraph* in March 1960: 'Some British industries, and they include firms employing large groups of workers, lead the world in enterprise in production methods, design, and salesmanship. Yet their relations with labour from the shop floor to the top are archaic.

'Their magnificent machines are nursed, maintained, and cared for day and night. But the human element is treated in an astonishingly off-hand way. And without the man the machine could not be kept running. There are old-fashioned employers who believe the trade unions are just a damned nuisance and avoid any dealings with them for as long as possible. There are firms which tolerate and only just tolerate unions.

'There are firms which, at the first hearing of a workers' claim, say "no" automatically. There are those which delay negotiations interminably. Some lay off, swiftly and unnecessarily, workers on all departments when there is only a small strike in one department. The firms may think that this will alienate the innocent workers against the strikes. Sometimes it does, but the move is often seen through by the workers and the net result is a rallying of all the men behind the strike. Then there are firms which surrender too readily to noisy shop stewards. . . .

'Lack of communications between management and men, about reasons for changes in production methods, the transfer of workers, redundancy, and so on, provide the grounds for trouble. All these and other factors tend, rightly or wrongly, to create bloody-mindedness among the workers. The atmosphere is soured. Then, when there is a dispute over a particular issue, the men boil over and the unions are blamed for not controlling their members.

'Too often there are strikes over the flimsiest of pretexts. But they would never have occurred at all if there had not been a backlog of unsettled and not-forgotten grievances.'

This kind of thing has undoubtedly contributed to the troubles in many motor firms, which have contrasted so strikingly with the comparative peace and spirit of cooperation at Vauxhall Motors, in spite of the fact that they pay lower wages than most of their rivals in the Midlands. The main difference at Vauxhall Motors is that an enlightened management has paid great attention to labour relations over a long period of years. They have also succeeded in integrating the shop stewards' movement into their consultative machinery through the elected management advisory committee, which is a really effective working body exercising influence over a wide range of subjects including the grading of workers,

The fact that they work on time rates instead of piece rates may help, but their tradition of good relations was established before the bonus system was ended. Moreover the time rate system at Ford Motors has not prevented frequent trouble.

Another factor which constantly operates against good labour relations in British industry is the systematic refusal of employers, except public employers, to recognize trade unions unless they are forced to do so. The battles which most manual works won years ago still have to be fought by white-collar unions.

Outstanding examples of this attitude are in banks and insurance. In both many, though not all, of the employers set up their own sponsored house associations and refuse to recognize the unions, even where they are more representative, or to negotiate with them.

The National Union of Bank Employees is a rapidly growing union with more than 50,000 members which has for years been campaigning for recognition by all means short of a strike. Repeatedly they have sought the assistance of the Minister of Labour, without avail. Their propaganda is continuous. At the end of 1960 they even became involved in a strike in the Derby Trustee Savings Bank.

The engineering employers try to prevent the organization of supervisors by sponsoring and helping the Foremen and Staff Mutual Benefit Society, membership of which confers attractive benefits, is confined to non-unionists, and is often made a condition of promotion. Members of the Clerical and Administrative Workers' Union employed by the Automobile Association took part in a strike in Birmingham at the end of 1960, after which the association proceeded to set up a house society. Footballers were able to do nothing about their feudal conditions of employment until their strike threat at the beginning of 1961. Distributive workers only began to secure recognition by the chain and multiple stores when they could show that they were strong enough to use industrial action.

One or more of the unions puts down a resolution for the Trades Union Congress every year. It is an annual reminder to the leaders of all the unions that, however much employers may pay lip service to the principles of cooperation and free negotiation, it remains true that the only way a union can secure recognition and fair treatment is by the power and will of its members to strike.

Perhaps the most fundamental failure of the employers in the post-war period, however, has been their refusal to take the unions into partnership in a joint effort to make British industry efficient and prosperous. Yet employers are always saying that it is misleading to talk about the 'two sides' in industry, and that employers and workers have a common interest in increasing production and reducing costs. That is basically true, of course. But when the opportunity came under the Labour Government to make the unions real partners in the conduct of industry it was rejected.

It is not the first time they have turned down such an opportunity. After the General Strike of 1926 a group of twenty leading industrialists led by Sir Alfred Mond (Lord Melchett) invited the T.U.C. leaders to meet them and the invitation was accepted. Walter Citrine then said the unions were ready to participate actively 'in a concerted effort to raise industry to its highest efficiency by developing the most scientific methods of production, eliminating waste and harmful restrictions, removing causes of friction and avoidable conflict, and promoting the largest possible output so as to provide a rising standard of life and continuously improving conditions of employment'.

The T.U.C. General Council reported to the union executives in 1928: 'For the first time in history the representatives of organized labour have been invited to meet a group of important industrialists to discuss the finance and management of industry; new developments in technology and organization; the organization of industry itself, nationally and internationally; means for ensuring the status and security of workers; and methods of achieving the highest possible standard of living for all. These are the things the trade union movement has been claiming for years to have some voice in, and for years it has been denied that voice.'

A conference took place and a joint committee drew up recommendations for the creation of a National Industrial Council representing both sides of industry and charged with the appointment of joint conciliation boards to deal with disputes which the normal machinery in any industry failed to settle. A statement also dealt with the more rational organization of industry and provision for displaced workers.

Meetings then took place between the T.U.C. and the Federation of British Industries and the National Confederation of Employers (as it was then) and periodic consultations between the three bodies were agreed upon. There was little result, however. The two employers' organizations were reluctant from the beginning. Neither of them accepted the recommendations of the joint conference and the proposed National Industrial Council never met.

Even earlier, the Whitley Councils set up in many industries at the end of and after the First World War might have been made the basis of real cooperation, as they were in one or two industries, but probably neither side was ready for it then.

The most formidable reactionary obstacle to such a partnership is perhaps the great Engineering and Allied Employer's National Federation, with forty-six local associations and 4300 member firms employing nearly 2,000,000 people. Defence of the prerogatives of management has always been their highest priority. Their two biggest disputes, in 1897 and 1922, were both lock-outs to stop trade unions from what they regarded as interference. They won both. After the first the settlement said: 'The federation employers, while disavowing any intention of interfering with the proper functions of trade unions, will admit no interference with the management in their business.' The settlement in 1922 used the now familiar words: 'The employers have the right to manage their establishments and the trade unions have the right to exercise their functions.' A meaningless phrase – since the exercising of trade union functions inevitably limits the authority of management – but still part of the agreement.

Since the Second World War the Engineering Employers' Federation have repeatedly rejected suggestions from the unions and recommendations by courts of inquiry that they should set up a joint council or some similar joint body. There will be no partnership with the unions if they can help it.

It may not be easy to recapture the opportunity that was thrown away during the immediate post-war years. The Labour Government was then endeavouring to develop a system of joint endeavour from top to bottom of industry on the lines set down by the T.U.C. in their interim report on post-war reconstruction. The union leaders were ready to play their part. But the employers, though they were willing to join with the unions in any joint body which was confined to talking and giving advice, from the National Joint Advisory Council to the British Productivity Council, resisted with the utmost determination any proposal which gave the unions any share in authority.

The centre of the new pattern, as the Government and T.U.C. saw it, was the provision for development councils in each industry to exercise supervision over it. The employers would not have it. In spite of their resistance, a few were set up during the Labour Government, but were rapidly dissolved when the Conservatives were returned to power. The unions wanted the planning board, the National Production Advisory Council on Industry, the regional councils to be really constructive joint bodies. The employers showed little interest. Some employers' associations will not even allow the unions to be represented on their research organizations.

Apart from the development councils, the place where responsibility could really be shared was in the factories, on the joint consultative committees, but in many firms (though not all) they were allowed to languish. Too many were confined to social matters or used to inform the union representatives of decisions already taken in the hope that they would help to put them into effect smoothly. Responsibility without power or influence is no more likely to appeal to workers than anybody else.

A booklet entitled *Understanding Labour Relations*, issued by the Institute of Directors in 1958, warned employers that if acceptance of joint consultation was too long delayed it might well be enforced by law. 'The climate of opinion is turning towards acceptance of the view that management must seek the active cooperation of its employees and, by putting them in the picture, command their interest as well as their labour . . . an extension of joint consultation will reduce friction and disputes and win the interest and support of workpeople.' But putting them in the picture is not enough. They must help to draft the designs.

In September 1960, the National Union of Manufacturers, grown tired of bitterness and strikes, produced a document called the *British Charter of Industrial Relations,* aimed at uniting all concerned in industry into a working partnership with the objectives of industrial peace, expanding trade abroad, and rising standards of living at home.

They advocated more effective joint industrial councils, more security for workers, and better treatment when redundancy is unavoidable. They proposed the establishment of a national conciliation council, local arbitrating bodies, and the appointment of a special Registrar of Trade Unions.

Much of the document was trite and some of it ill-conceived, but it was an attempt to find a fresh approach and it might have been supposed that other organizations concerned with industrial relations, such as the British Employers' Confederation, the T.U.C., and the Ministry of Labour, would at least have recognized it as such. In practice everybody ignored it.

The N.U.M. had committed the heinous offence of trespassing on the territory of the B.E.C., which is recognized as the one central employers' body which deals with industrial relations.

Some employers fear that these things are a stage on the way to workers' control. There are a few employers' organizations which work very closely with the unions. There are employers who have developed joint consultation to a point where the workers really have a say in everything that goes on, but they are few. Other employers have developed schemes of 'copartnership' and profit-sharing, but the majority of them have stopped short of any real partnership.

Had the employers been willing to cooperate with the Labour Government and the unions a dozen years ago, the spirit in British industry might be very different today.

11

PRESCRIPTIONS

Twenty-three Complaints – Twenty-six Cures –
But the Patient Won't Take Any of Them

WE have said that the unions still do a good job over the greater part of British industry, but that the movement as a whole has lost its drive and sense of direction. As a result, serious weaknesses and occasional abuses have developed unchecked. We must now ask what can be done by the unions themselves, by the employers, and by the Government to remedy those weaknesses and abuses.

To help us look at the problem as a whole, here is a list of the main criticisms that have been made or mentioned (but not necessarily accepted by the author as justified) in the preceding chapters:

CHAPTER 1

1. Union leaders are underpaid and overworked.
2. Unions employ too few experts.
3. Members of the T.U.C. General Council are overloaded with responsibilities.

CHAPTER 2

4. Union dues are too low.
5. There is little tactical coordination of policy.
6. The unions make little or no attempt to work out a long-term policy.

CHAPTER 3

7. They have not thought out the consequences of their Socialist aims.
8. The link with the Labour party causes difficulties in relations with Governments and alienates many white-collar workers.

CHAPTER 4

9. The structure of the movement is out of date.

10. Union rivalries sometimes cause major strikes.

11. Union demarcation rules and agreements damage industry.

12. Recruitment is neglected.

CHAPTER 5

13. Management and union authority have broken down in some undertakings and the number of unofficial strikes is excessive.

CHAPTER 6

14. Apathy among members has allowed Communists to establish a minority control of some union organizations.

15. Election malpractices occur in some unions.

CHAPTER 7

16. Vindictive action is sometimes taken against those who do not take part in strikes.

17. The closed shop restricts individual freedom.

18. The Bridlington Agreement may prevent workers from belonging to the union of their choice.

19. Unrecognized unions are sometimes prevented from carrying out their functions.

20. The largest unions wield excessive power through the block vote at the Trades Union Congress and Labour party conference.

CHAPTER 8

21. Restrictive labour practices reduce output.

22. Not enough effort is made by unions to convince members that their interests require maximum efficiency.

CHAPTER 9

23. Unions devote insufficient attention to public relations and internal communications.

The importance one attaches to these various criticisms and the kind of remedies advocated naturally depend on one's conception of the role which trade unions should play in the modern industrial society. Perhaps therefore I should begin by explaining my own assumptions.

First of all, it seems to me probable that full employment or near full employment will be maintained most of the time. If this expectation proves unfounded, the future system I envisage would not be essential, though I would still regard it as desirable. But at any rate a high level of employment is an aim of all political parties, so that it is reasonable to base one's hopes for the trade unions on the assumption that it will be maintained.

If there is full employment, then wide variations in wages cannot continue for long, because an industry must pay high enough wages to keep a labour force. That is why a wage increase in one industry since the war has regularly been followed by increases in other industries. The ability of an industry to pay is largely immaterial since an industry must pay enough to get labour if it is to exist.

Except in its details, the thing is inevitable and automatic. After a pattern-making settlement, sometimes during it, the fierce challenges of union leaders and the stern resistance of employer are intended mainly to impress their own supporters and the national audience – rather like the shouts and groans of all-in wrestlers. Sometimes the leaders in negotiations have an understanding before they begin as to what the ultimate result will be. The most a union can hope for is to get a shilling or two more than its rival, which will probably be lost again in the next round.

It is true that workers in some industries, like railways and agriculture, keep lagging behind, losing their best young workers in the process, but eventually they have to be dragged forward again, not only because the loss of workers becomes insupportable but also because there is a strong public sense that it is unjust for any group of workers to be underpaid compared with others. 'The feeling that wages are a matter of social justice rather than mainly a function of customers' demand is now very deeply ingrained', lamented the *Economist*. The only result of the process is to make the labour force in those industries, increasingly composed of the old and unenterprising, restless and discontented so that they grow more and more inefficient and less and less likely to recover their place in the competitive world.

The economics of full employment and the sentiment of the public combine to impose the doctrine that the labourer is worthy of his hire, in other words that the price of a worker's skill and brawn and other qualities should be about the same to any industry for comparable jobs. There should be a price for a worker's skill, just as there is a price for raw materials, and if an employer cannot pay it then he should go out of business (unless it is necessary to keep him in business in the national interest by subsidies).

No doubt competitive bidding, particularly in fringe benefits, will continue to make jobs in the most prosperous industries relatively attractive, but that is rather a different matter from attempting to relate wage rates to ability to pay, and within limits is desirable as an aid to the transfer of labour from contracting to expanding industries.

If my line of argument is accepted as valid, it must have a profound effect on one's conception of the future functions of trade unions and the way in which they should now be developing. If there is to be in effect a national rate for comparable jobs, as to some extent there already is, then the shadow-boxing of competitive wage claims, on which unions and employers' organizations now spend much of their time and energy, is useless. Indeed it does harm, because it distracts them from much more important tasks, such as helping to increase output and smooth out the multifarious points of friction.

The basic issue is the national wage movement, and it is crazy to decide it by the chance outcome of a battle in one pattern-setting industry. It should be a matter for consideration by Government, employers, and T.U.C. together. This would rule out strikes over general wage movements, since you cannot stop the whole of industry. But agreements about wages movements could well be possible if they were made part of agreements about movements in personal incomes generally.

It would mean giving much greater authority to the T.U.C. but individual unions would still have work to do in seeing how such agreements were implemented in their industries, and strikes over such matters might well occur, at least for a time. But, with a general standard to interpret, most disputes could be settled by arbitration. In any case unions would be able to do much more to raise the living standards of their members, as they could even now, by cooperating to increase output. But there again their effectiveness depends on the willingness of employers to take them into partnership in the conduct of industry at all levels.

I have not, in considering present problems, assumed that any system like this is immediately possible. We will inevitably move in that direction, in practice if not in theory, so long as full employment continues, but unfortunately labour relations have been going backwards instead of forwards in the past ten years. It is as well to look for solutions of our problems, however, which will help us to move as rapidly as possible towards what seems to me the inevitable and essential future pattern.

I believe that the T.U.C. were on the right lines when they looked into the future in 1944. If the report on trade union structure and closer unity had been implemented, much of the recent conflict within the movement would have been avoided. The strengthening of the federations and joint bodies, and their close association with the General Council would have enabled the T.U.C. at least to make a beginning to giving effective leadership to the movement.

Implementation of the report on post-war reconstruction would have enabled employers and unions to get together, in the interests of all, on a national industrial council, on industrial boards for individual industries, and on effectual works councils in the undertakings. It is true that the report failed to deal adequately with wage-fixing, and there are other sections that would now be questioned; but it was on the right lines.

Since I accept much of the T.U.C.'s own conception of the movement's future, it follows that I find cause for criticism mainly where the trade unions have failed to implement their own principles and plans or where they seem to me to have failed to follow them to their logical conclusion. In some cases their failure raises the question whether they can be relied upon to remedy the defects that have appeared or whether it is advisable for the Government to take some action.

We can now go on to examine in turn the criticisms on our list and consider what, if anything, needs to be done about them.

1. *Union leaders are underpaid and overworked.*

The first thing to do is to pay men at the top, the executive heads of great organizations, salaries somewhat nearer the rate for the job, and do the same for the full-time officials at every union level. A trade union career must be made sufficiently attractive for a man of ability to enter upon it without having to impose a big financial sacrifice upon himself and his family.

His standard of life should not be so different from those of the representatives of employers and nationalized industries, and Civil Servants, with whom he has to deal. He should not always have the exasperating knowledge at the back of his mind, if he is an able man, that he can double or treble his salary by going outside the movement.

British trade unionists are singularly mean-spirited in their attitude to the pay of their officials. They expect them to work long hours without overtime, demand their presence at week-ends, give them a half or a third of what they are worth, and then attack them for not giving better service. The members want all that can be got for themselves in return for a niggardly contribution but expect their leaders to be motivated only by loyalty and a desire to serve the movement.

Perhaps there is a fear that if there is too much difference between the salary of a union leader and that of a working man, the leader will forget what it feels like to be a manual worker on a manual worker's wage. Leaders should remember, he perhaps thinks, that one of the oldest aims of the union movement has been greater equality. Perhaps he just does not want to shell out his coppers.

Whatever the reasons, it is working out badly for the unions.

They have got to compete for their officers with the other opportunities open to young men in the post-war world. There is hardly a student of the trade union movement who has not advocated better pay for the officers. They themselves, many of them, feel the need, but it is difficult for them to press it. Perhaps they should form a union.

Unions should double the salaries of all the officers of manual workers' unions immediately.

The salaries of officers in some but not all non-manual unions need the same treatment. Some salaries need more than doubling.

To raise the quality of union leaders it is necessary not only to attract men of the right calibre but also to make the most of them. That means more training and better training. The unions have been expanding their trade union educational facilities fairly rapidly, and at the time of writing are making another attempt to rationalize the facilities provided by various organizations. But they are not moving fast enough and they have not succeeded in getting sufficient response from the membership. While the T.U.C. college at Congress House was a substantial step forward, Britain must now be one of the few countries in Europe without a residential trade union college

Unions should double the facilities for trade union education.

2. *Unions employ too few experts.*

Increases in the pay of union officials would make it possible to offer more attractive salaries to the back-room boys. Nothing could do more to relieve the burden on union officials than an improvement in the number and quality of the economists, research staff, public relations experts, production engineers, lawyers, and others needed to advise the T.U.C. and individual unions, both at their headquarters and in the districts.

As has been pointed out, the two biggest unions and many others have no public relations departments. Only a handful of unions have research departments worth the name. Some rely on the Communist-dominated Labour Research Department. Their financial affairs are often conducted in an amateurish sort of way.

The T.U.C. have a good staff but too small to serve the movement as a whole, and their brightest young men sometimes leave for better paid employment.

The unions should employ a larger number of expert staff.

3. *Members of the T.U.C. General Council are overloaded with responsibilities.*

To relieve the pressure on members of the General Council, it is desirable that there should be appointed a full-time president and a number of full-time members who would relinquish their jobs with their own unions to devote their whole time to the work of the T.U.C. They would not be influenced, as every member now must be, by the special interests of their own union, but would be able to take a detached view of the movement as a whole.

They could well take over the chairmanships of the chief T.U.C. committees – finance and general purposes, economic, international, organization, production, social insurance, and press and publicity. The last-named should be one of the chief committees. It is assumed that trade union education will be under a special body. If the president took over the finance and general purposes, as the chairman does now, that would mean six additional full-time members, who with the president, general secretary, and assistant general secretary, could act as an inner council or executive.

At present the only full-time member of the council is the general secretary. The heads of departments act as secretaries to the various committees, but have of course much less standing, particularly in the public eye, than a full-time chairman would. It might well be that outstanding members of the staff would sometimes be elected to the council.

I assume that the full-time members would be elected, though not annually. Five-year terms of office would give them a more reasonable sense of security.

The Amalgamated Engineering Union put to the 1947 Congress the suggestion that all or a number of the members of the General Council should be engaged full-time on the T.U.C., but were overwhelmingly defeated after it had been argued on behalf of

the General Council that the effect would be t
ional body with a degree of bureaucratic aut
lead to the negation of democracy.

Ultimate power, however, would remain wit
The full-time members could give new vigour to
of agreed policy, and, if the right men were cho
acquire considerable influence even without the
block vote behind them. That seems to have hap
countries, such as West Germany, where such sys
adopted. After all, Citrine had no block vote behi

Moreover one could mention numerous examp
of small unions who have exercised great influence
their personal qualities. Sir Alfred Roberts, for ins
45,000 votes are neither here nor there, had undisput
on social insurance, when he was chairman of that
and on the International Labour Organization. He
like him have devoted so much time to General Co
that they have been in effect half-time but unpaid m
could only strengthen the Council for them to be give
positions. The real objection, I think, is the fear that
increase the authority of the T.U.C.

*Unions should add a full-time president and six full-time m
the T.U.C. General Council.*

4. *Union dues are too low.*

The suggestions so far, and some still to come, will cost
It has been pointed out that union dues are proportic
much smaller than before the war. They are insufficient ei
build up adequate funds for industrial disputes, or to pay o
adequate salaries, or to extend trade union education suffici
or to provide the necessary expert advice, or to provid
T.U.C. with the resources it needs.

Union dues should be doubled.

5. *There is little tactical coordination of policy.*

I described in Chapter 2 how the trade union movement in
past few years has been straining towards some degree of
ordination of industrial policy. The drive has come from

centre, represented by Mr Birch, and from the left, represented by Mr Foulkes, but it has got nowhere in the T.U.C. because the individual unions refuse to relinquish any part of their autonomy. At the time of writing, Mr Birch's resolution, adopted at the 1959 Congress, has not been fully considered by the General Council. What he suggested was that there should be consultations between the General Council and the executives of unions before policy-making union delegates conferences.

That appears to be a reasonable beginning, but if it is to have any effect, then the General Council must first discuss tactical policy on wages, hours, and other matters for the movement as a whole. That would mean either that these things should be considered regularly by the economic committee or that they should set up a special wages committee, comparable to that of the British Employers' Confederation.

'What happens in one industry has an immediate repercussion on another,' said a B.E.C. booklet on its structure and work in 1959. 'The importance to employers of exchanging views and notifying one another of their intentions is therefore obvious.'

One might have supposed that the importance to unions would have been equally obvious. The balance of advantage would seem to be in entrusting the task to the T.U.C. economic committee, since it does in any case consider the general economic background on which policy and conditions must be based.

The T.U.C. General Council should regularly discuss tactical plans for the industrial policy of the movement.

It may be questioned whether the General Council is sufficiently representative for this purpose. The problem would be simplified if the unions were to carry out the proposals of the 1944 interim report on trade union structure and closer unity, regarding the strengthening of federations and their closer links with the General Council. Something will be said about that later when we come to discuss criticisms of trade union structure. But until those proposals are carried out, if they ever are, it might well be found advisable for the economic committee or the General Council to bring representatives of the main federations and negotiating bodies into their discussions.

It would all obviously be very difficult so long as the union leaders are so divided and lacking in central leadership as they have been since the end of the Arthur Deakin triumvirate. Indeed it is very difficult for the General Council to do anything worthwhile. A group of full-time General Council members, such as has been suggested, might well give the kind of central leadership that is needed, but unfortunately there is little prospect at present that such a group will be appointed.

6. *The unions make little or no attempt to work out long-term policy.*

Examples of important trade union issues which have been neglected are wages policy in full employment, wage settlement in publicly owned industries, workers' participation in control, redundancy, compulsory arbitration, and strikes. We are concerned here with strategic policy, as opposed to the coordination of tactical policy we have just discussed. This is not the place to examine what trade union policies on these issues should be, but I explained in Chapter 2 why it seems to me desirable for the trade union movement to have an agreed policy on them.

I should like to see the General Council think out again the basic purposes of the movement, as comprehensively as they did in the interim report on post-war reconstruction, and in some respects more comprehensively.

A lot has happened since 1944. The industrial environment has changed. The movement's old direction has been lost and no new one found. It cannot go on indefinitely stumbling blindly onwards.

The General Council should prepare a comprehensive report on the policy and aims of the trade union movement.

So far as wages policy is concerned, the proposals made for the coordination of union policy, while they might do much to harmonize rival and competitive claims, are not enough. Wages cannot be considered in a vacuum. The unions gain little by forcing up wages to an extent that forces up prices, but they cannot be expected to hold back unless other sections of the community also do so. A wages policy is impossible without a policy on other incomes. The obvious conclusion is that there should be consultation between the Government and the T.U.C. over the whole range of personal incomes.

That may not be possible with a Conservative Government. If not, then the present struggles will have to be continued, with the greater degree of method and common sense that would result if the trade unions coordinated their policy. It would relieve the continual uncertainty about wage costs if long-term agreements became the rule rather than the exception, as they have done in the United States.

Employers and unions in all industries should consider the possibility of long-term wage agreements.

Though any effective consultation on personal incomes may be impossible with a Conservative Government, it would be essential if a Labour Government were to be returned with a determination to keep a closer control over the economy. One of the most important parts of the suggested report would be a plan for dealing with these questions when and if Labour returns to office. The vague assurances in T.U.C. statements suggest that the trade unions would be prepared to cooperate, but there is need to think out how it should be done. At present the Labour party dare not attempt that for fear of offending the unions, and the T.U.C. regard the question as one for Government initiative.

The settlement of wages in publicly owned industries is a particular aspect of the problem which needs to be dealt with urgently. The London busmen's strike in 1958 was a warning, so far ignored, of the danger of wage disputes in nationalized industries giving rise to major struggles between the Government and the trade union movement.

One solution would be to give public boards complete independence of the Government in their labour policy. They could then conduct their struggles with the unions just like private employers. But they would not be personally affected financially by a dispute, as private employers are. Moreover it would be very hard for a Government to give so much freedom to an industry like public transport, which is not paying its way and is therefore dependent on the government to finance wage increases. It is also perhaps expecting too much of a Government that it should not use its influence on public boards when it is bending every effort to restrain an inflationary situation.

Moreover most industries under public ownership are basic industries or services. The pressure of a strike is imposed less by making the employer lose money than by damaging the national economy and causing inconvenience and loss to the general public. On the whole it seems to be desirable that the right to call a national strike should be abandoned in publicly owned industries. But if that is done, then it is essential that the workers should be assured of fair treatment as compared with those in private industry.

The right to strike has in fact been relinquished in theory in most nationalized industries whose agreements make provision for final and binding arbitration in the event of failure to agree. Such agreements apply to electricity supply, gas, British Road Services, and civil air transport. A similar agreement applied to coal mining until 1961.

In those industries which depend on arbitration, it is usual for changes in wages and conditions to follow those in outside industry, either through negotiated agreements or through arbitration. But if arbitrators take into account the financial position of the undertaking, as the non-binding arbitration on railway wages has sometimes done, the workers may get a raw deal.

There is a strong case for extending the Civil Service principle of fair comparison with pay in outside industry, with arbitration as a last resort, to the nationalized industries, and indeed to public employment generally, in spite of the arguments against this advanced by the T.U.C. General Council in their 1960 report.

The case is particularly strong in non-profit-making public employment, for instance in the health service, local government, the schools, and fire and police services, but the difficulty of finding comparable occupations would be an obstacle for some of them. It might be possible to overcome that by using one of the systems of job evaluation.

It may be objected that commercial undertakings such as mines and railways should take account of the profitability of the concern. But the Post Office does not do so. In times of full employment or near full employment they have in any case to pay rates comparable with those outside if they are to maintain adequate manpower, and to keep dragging behind only causes unrest, as it has done on the railways.

It is in the interest of the trade unions to establish these principles, because they would benefit most members and avoid the danger of battles with the Government which they do not want and are bound to lose.

Trade unions should press for the Civil Service principle of fair comparison with pay in outside industry, including final resort to binding arbitration, to be applied to all public employment.

An incidental effect of the struggles between the Government and the unions in 1957 and 1958 was to demonstrate how difficult it is for a Government at the same time to pursue an active wages policy and to operate the conciliation machine, the object of which should be simply to help the two sides of industry to settle their disputes peacefully. The Minister of Labour was placed in an impossible position, and it was several times evident, particularly during the London bus strike, that the conciliators were being so influenced to do nothing that might result in a wage increase that they could not carry out their traditional impartial function. Yet a Government these days must have a wages policy.

The objection is particularly great in public employment, where formally or informally the Government is on one side in the negotiations but is at the same time acting as mediator between the two sides. If pay in public employment were fixed on the Civil Service principle, the objection would be less but would not be removed. The task of conciliation can only be carried out impartially by completely independent people.

The conciliation machinery of the Ministry of Labour should be transferred to the Industrial Court or some other independent body.

It was suggested in Chapter 2 that the unions should clear their minds on their attitude towards compulsory arbitration. During the last few years, it was recalled, many of the strongest unions have rejected offers by the employers to settle their disputes by arbitration while at the same time the T.U.C. has been complaining because the Government rescinded the Industrial Disputes Order with its provision for compulsory arbitration. They complained because the order was valuable to unions lacking the power or the will to strike.

We have already suggested that binding arbitration should be the final resort for all public employees. The principle they would be interpreting in that case would be clear – the principle that their pay should bear fair comparison with that of comparable jobs in outside industry.

But arbitrators on wage claims in private industry have no similar yardstick. They cannot merely compare everybody's wages with everybody else's. They have at present no precise terms of reference to guide them. There is no agreement as to the relative importance to be attached to the various factors taken into consideration, such as the effect on the national economy, the ability of the industry to pay, the cost of living, and wage movements in other industries.

If the time ever comes when the general lines of wage movements are agreed nationally between the Government and the T.U.C., or by any other means, it might well be argued that the application of such agreements to particular industries or occupations should be settled by arbitration. But anything of that kind is a long way off.

As things are there is no satisfactory alternative to the present arrangement, under which employers give as little as they can and unions get a much as they can, both with the thought very much in their minds of what might happen if it came to a trial of strength. The results have no relation to the national interest or natural justice or any other principle. Sometimes the result is a strike, but the strikes are comparatively few and we must just make the best of it.

None of the various suggestions, like a cooling off period before a strike can begin or a compulsory strike ballot, have much to commend them.

It is sometimes said that disputes are settled round the table anyway, so they might as well be settled that way before as after a strike, but that is unrealistic. Settlements are much influenced by a knowledge that a strike is possible and may be influenced, one way or the other, by an actual strike.

It is also sometimes said that organizations are now so big, and the country's economy so hard-pressed, that we cannot afford big strikes. Certainly it would be nice if we could do without them. But so far we have afforded them. Unless some agreed national wages policy can be devised, the right to strike must be maintained. The weak unions who cry out for compulsory arbitration will have to accept the fact that to secure fair settlements, often even to secure recognition, they will have to prove that they have the will and the power to strike. That has always been true and remains so.

So far as sympathetic strikes are concerned, circumstances vary so much that it is impossible to make any universal rule, but there are obviously strong arguments, from everybody's point of view, against spreading a dispute so that a comparatively minor affair is turned into a major struggle. It is equally clearly undesirable that workers should break agreements with employers with whom they have no dispute and who are in no way concerned with the origins of the trouble. The question should be given full consideration in the inquiry which, I shall suggest later on, should be held to examine the possibility of making collective agreements legally binding.

Nothing I said earlier was meant to suggest that arbitration has no place in the settlement of disputes in private industry. Once the pattern of a new round of wage settlements has been set by one or more of the major industries, others may well go to arbitration if they cannot agree on its application to them, as they usually can. They would be encouraged to do so if they knew how arbitrators came to their decisions (for the pattern of wage movements is not and should not be a series of parallel lines) and if the awards of the various arbitrators were more consistent.

The Government should give the Industrial Court the responsibility of bringing together arbitrators and independent members of wage-fixing bodies to draw up a consistent policy and arbitrators should give reasons for their decisions.

In drawing up their policy, the arbitrators would no doubt seek the views of all interested parties, including the Government and the representative bodies of the two sides of industry.

The result of this would be that arbitration awards would become more predictable. In time arbitration might be used increasingly for pattern-making settlements, as courts of inquiry (which gave reasons for their recommendations) have sometimes been used. The reference tribunal for the coal industry gives its reasons and the Industrial Court used to give reasons in its early days, but few tribunals do so now.

An important reason why the Industrial Court and some others no longer give reasons is that the chairman sits with two other members of a panel, one an employer and one a trade unionist. These two are often willing to put their names to an arbitrary decision, when they would not be prepared to put their names to the reasons for it. The way out of this is to have single arbitrators with advisers instead of three-man courts.

All disputes about the interpretation of agreements should of course be settled by arbitration, but they are not a frequent source of trouble on a national scale. Strikes resulting from union rivalry and unofficial strikes are dealt with below.

7. *The unions have not thought out the consequences of their Socialist aims.*

Perhaps one ought to add 'if any' to this criticism, in spite of their constitutions. But if their attitude to public ownership is obscure, at least they believe in planning and they have never formally renounced their belief in workers' participation. For reasons that have been given, a great extension of public ownership, or real national planning, which would have to include wages or workers' participation that had some substance, would all profoundly affect the functions of trade unions. This too is a subject for the report on the broad policy and aims of the movement.

8. *The link with the Labour party causes difficulties in relations with Governments and alienates some white-collar workers.*

Whether or not the unions made a mistake in creating the Labour party is a question that could be debated at length. The present position is that no other party shares the views of the trade unions and that the Labour party would collapse without their support. The electorate may eventually decide that they would prefer two parties neither of which was so closely allied to a vested interest, but it cannot be said they are yet thinking that way in large numbers. The awkwardness of relations with Governments has not proved very serious.

As for the white-collar workers, the sense of grievance arising from their relative loss of status may well make them adopt a more active industrial policy, as some have already done, and as a result come closer in attitude to the manual workers. They are already closer in financial standing and in the fringe benefits which are so important a sign of status. If the trade unions can eliminate the abuses which create so much public hostility, they will be much more likely to absorb non-manual workers. The T.U.C. itself is already tending to weaken its links with the party and no doubt will continue to do so, but the case for an organic change is weak.

9. *The structure of the movement is out of date.*

This can hardly be questioned and is indeed accepted by the T.U.C. themselves. It is gradually being improved, but far too slowly to keep pace with industrial change. If one were starting afresh, one would probably build quite a differently shaped movement, as the West Germans did after the war; but as things are we must accept that it would be quite impracticable to, say, break up the big general and craft unions and replace them by industrial unions. The plans approved in 1944 were sensible and imaginative and (apart from some additional suggestions made elsewhere) I can think of nothing better.

The 1944 interim report on trade union structure and closer unity should be implemented.

How this is to be brought about is hard to say. The General Council put in a lot of hard work on it from 1945 to 1947 with meagre results. Perhaps the interval has been long enough to make it worthwhile starting on a new drive.

213

A beginning could be made by building up the proposed links between the T.U.C. and the federations, which could come about through the suggestion made earlier on about coordinating policy.

10. *Union rivalries sometimes cause major strikes.*

These usually arise when all the unions in an industry are not represented on a joint committee or federation which negotiates on their behalf. The railway unions are the most notorious example. There has also been trouble in more than one industry as a result of rivalry between maintenance craft unions and the productive workers, as in the newspaper strike of 1955. The dock strike of the same year also arose out of the demand of one union for representation on the joint Industrial Council. Implementation of the 1944 report would remove the causes of most such disputes.

There really does not seem to be anything to do about the railway unions except to wait for them to acquire sense. Modernization is making their rivalries more and more artificial. If the suggested wage policy for public employment were to be introduced, it would remove a major cause of conflict, but no doubt they would find others. Far too little is done by the T.U.C. to impress upon them that they are a discredit to the trade union movement. The power accorded to the General Council in 1955 to intervene in such disputes at an earlier stage has made little difference and seems unlikely to do so.

11. *Union demarcation rules and agreements damage industry.*

Strikes arising out of demarcation disputes have been one of the major causes of public reaction against the unions, mainly because of the apparent absurdity of some of those in ship-building. Actual strikes, however, are of less importance than the constant restriction on output in a few industries resulting from time-wasting demarcation lines and from long arguments as to who should do work which meanwhile remains undone.

This is a problem which goes deep into the history and structure of industries employing craftsmen. Amalgamations of craft unions would ease the situation; but even within a single union, for instance the boilermakers' society, there are disputes between different crafts. The only real solution is to remodel the whole basis of apprenticeship. The inadequacy of the Carr Committee's report on the training of young people was a great disappointment.

The present system produces men trained in a narrow range of work, which in some cases can hardly any longer be called skilled, and often inadequately trained even for that. The employers continue to recognize the men thus trained as craftsmen and to accept the rigid demarcation lines between them. Yet the tendency of modern industrial development is to blur the traditional distinction between the crafts or to replace skilled work by unskilled. The need is for craftsmen with a far wider range of skill in unions catering for a number of the occupations which are still treated as separate crafts.

Representatives of building unions met in London in April 1959 to discuss the impact and implications of new techniques and materials in the industry. The Amalgamated Society of Woodworkers accepted that developments on these lines would eventually be necessary, but thought that the technological change in building was in so early a stage that it was premature to suggest extensive amalgamation, though there might be a case for amalgamation of cognate trades. The Amalgamated Union of Building Trade Workers, on the other hand, and the documents prepared by the National Federation of Building Trade Operatives, suggested that change had gone far enough to justify examining the need for radical change in union structure and apprenticeship. There are those in printing, shipbuilding, and other industries who think likewise.

Government, employers, and unions together should remodel the apprenticeship system to eliminate its narrow craft basis.

Most demarcation disputes ought to be prevented by the machinery that already exists. What seems to be lacking is some organization in the regions which would have the responsibility of looking after the local interests of the trade union movement as a whole, not only by endeavouring to secure the reference of inter-union disputes to the appropriate machinery, but also by providing research and other services which are now lacking, inspiring recruitment campaigns, and so on. The federations or confederations concerned are too narrow for these purposes, which should be related to the wider movement.

There are two kinds of local organization connected with the T.U.C. – the regional advisory councils and the trades councils. There are twelve of the former and more than 500 of the latter, varying greatly in size and importance, linked together in federations, and associated with the T.U.C. General Council on a Trades Councils Joint Consultative Committee. The regional advisory councils are elected at an annual meeting in each region, with all full-time officers of affiliated unions entitled to attend. The trades councils consist of representatives of union branches in the localities.

The functions of the regional councils include the nomination of trade union representatives on regional boards for industry and other bodies, and the preparation of reports for the T.U.C. on the industrial situation in their region. For the purposes I have mentioned, the regional councils would appear to be most suitable. They would require to be strengthened by the provision by the T.U.C. of full-time officers who would provide the services needed by trade unions throughout the region.

The T.U.C. should strengthen their regional advisory councils by the provision of full-time staff to provide services to the movement throughout the region in the fields of research, recruitment, adjustment of inter-union difficulties, and so on.

12. *Recruitment is neglected.*

The large proportion of non-unionists is a continuing source of weakness to the unions. There should be an officer at Congress House whose sole responsibility it would be to organize and inspire recruitment campaigns where organization is weak, making full use of modern methods of publicity. He would work through the unions and through the strengthened regional advisory councils just mentioned. The suggested full-time chairman of the organization committee would fulfil this purpose.

13. *Management and union authority have broken down in some undertakings and the number of unofficial strikes is excessive.*

The General Council presented an interim report on this subject in 1960 and continued its investigations. The long-term answer is to aim at a workshop partnership between management and workers, with which it is essential that the union should be closely associated, with the object of improving efficiency and conditions to the maximum extent. That would have to start with a change of attitude on the part of most employers and a corresponding change in the attitude of workshop representatives.

The present position of the shop steward and joint shop stewards' committees, with little responsibility to anyone, either above or below them, encourages the formation of their little empires. But in modern conditions shop stewards are needed. The first essential is to integrate the whole shop steward system into the life of the plant and into the structure of the unions, and for management and unions to act firmly to prevent their exceeding the functions allotted to them. It will mean reorientating the local structure of many unions.

Trade unions should base their local structure so far as possible on the places where their members work rather than on the places where they live.

Trade unions and employers should closely define the functions of shop stewards and shop stewards' committees and act firmly to prevent their being exceeded.

The slowness of the machinery for dealing with disputes is undoubtedly one of the causes of unofficial strikes. The provisions for the avoidance of disputes in the engineering industry, for instance, are as follows:

Workers with a grievance take it up with their foreman. Failing agreement, they go with their shop steward to the shop manager. Failing agreement, they go to the joint works committee. Failing agreement, they go to a local conference between the local association and local representatives of the union within seven days of application. Failing agreement, they go to the Central Conference in York, which meets every month to consider cases referred to it up to fourteen days earlier. The Central Conference may make a recommendation or there may be a failure to agree. The agreement says that there shall be no stoppage of work until this procedure is carried through.

Many disputes are, of course, settled at an early stage, but if they go through to the Central Conference, the process takes several weeks with no assurance of a verdict at the end.

Mr B. C. Roberts suggests in *Trade Unions in a Free Society* (see Preface) that there is an extremely strong case for moving in the direction of the American system of workshop arbitration as the final stage of grievance procedure.

'In the United States', he writes, 'every collective contract makes provision for the private arbitration of disputes. There are more than 30,000 arbitrators who are regularly called upon to settle questions in dispute.'

A difficulty in the way of adopting the system in Britain is that we have no detailed written contracts, as the Americans have, for arbitrators to interpret. Mr Roberts says that the first step to be taken is the codifying of company rules and practices in a written document, as the Ministry of Labour suggested in its pamphlet *Positive Employment Policies*. Even without that development, there is much to be said for using this method to deal with local disputes which have no wider implications. It may be noted that the recent demarcation agreement between the boilermakers and the shipwrights made provision for local arbitration.

Procedures for the settlement of disputes should be revised to provide for local disputes to be settled at workshop level, by independent arbitration when necessary.

Frequent unofficial strikes are normally a symptom of bad labour relations and of the loss of union authority. If the causes we have been discussing were removed, the symptoms might be expected gradually to wane. But there has been a good deal of discussion also about repressing the symptoms.

The group of Conservative lawyers who produced *A Giant's Strength* (see Preface) advocated that a strike in breach of union

218

rules should be illegal and that the union, or persons calling such a strike, should lose the protection given by the various Acts to trade unions. But the enforcement of union rules is surely a matter for the union, not for the law. Moreover, it is at least questionable whether it is desirable to repress unofficial strikes altogether. In the big unions of today there are often sections of workers who feel that their interests are neglected and that there is no other way to secure what they regard as their just rights than to strike. If such strikes were repressed by law, union officials might feel it much less necessary to protect the interests of minorities.

But unofficial strikes usually break not only the rules of the union but also the agreed procedure for the avoidance of disputes. There is a much stronger case for making strikes in breach of collective agreements illegal, both official strikes and unofficial strikes. There can be no justification for deliberately flouting agreements as the National Union of Railwaymen threatened to do in February 1960.

At present collective agreements are generally regarded as binding 'in honour only'. The whole of the collective bargaining system, according to the Ministry of Labour's *Industrial Relations Handbook*, 'rests upon the principal of mutual consent, and the value of the agreements and the machinery for settling disputes has depended upon the loyal acceptance by the constituent members on both sides of the decisions reached. This acceptance is purely voluntary, depending solely on the sense of moral obligation. Loyal acceptance has in fact been the rule in all the trades concerned. Although the question has been raised from time to time of the adequacy of these methods, the view has always been taken that it was not desirable to adopt some alternative based upon principles other than that of mutual consent or to introduce any system of penalties for non-observance of agreements.'

However, there is some difference of opinion among authorities on trade union law as to whether collective agreements are only binding in honour in all circumstances, though in practice they are so treated.

Breaches of agreements by workers or unions are usually by failing to carry out the procedure laid down for the avoidance of disputes, whereas breaches by an employer would usually be by failing to observe agreements on wages and conditions. There have been a number of Acts to compel employers, including those not party to the agreement, to observe agreed conditions, the latest of them the 1959 Terms and Conditions of Employment Act, but there has been no legislation to compel unions to observe disputes procedure. In those countries where collective agreements are binding in law, unofficial strikes are much fewer than in Britain and deliberate breach of a contract by a major union would be unthinkable.

If the big unions in this country were to make a practice of ignoring their collective agreements, the whole system would clearly be in danger of breaking down unless it *were* given legal backing, enabling both associations and individual employers to take action for breach of agreements. No one would be happy if the much-vaunted voluntary system had to be abandoned, but it obviously could become necessary. Whether it has already become necessary is a matter which requires careful study.

An inquiry should be held into the implications of making collective agreements legally binding on trade unions, employers, employers' associations, and their members.

To make them binding on unions and employers would obviously be practicable, though not necessarily desirable, but to make them binding on individual members of unions would present the same kind of problems as arise from proposals to forbid unofficial strikes as such.

14. *Apathy among members has allowed Communists to establish a minority control in some union organizations*

The ideal cure for the Communist problem is for more members to take an interest in the affairs of their union, since the Communists are in a very small minority everywhere. Perhaps more could be done by the leadership to make trade unionists aware of the methods and policy of the Communist party. The suggested extension of trade union education would help.

Whether it is desirable to exclude Communists from holding office, as the Transport and General Workers' Union did, has been much debated. It is an infringement of democracy to deprive electors of a free choice and there is always the danger that the Communists will go underground. There can be no objection, however, to insistence that Communist candidates should disclose the fact. Some union rules prevent this being done, on the grounds that the industrial record of the candidate is alone relevant.

All unions should make it a rule that candidates for office disclose their political affiliations.

Mr Woodrow Wyatt, who has made a study of Communist activities, contends in *The Peril in our Midst* (1956) that the success of the Communists is partly the fault of the Labour party.

'The Labour party should summon, from all over the country, regional and district conferences to which representatives of unions affiliated to the Labour party should be invited. The Labour party should point out that trade unions contribute large funds to the Labour party – presumably because they agree with its policies. Why then, it should be asked, are they letting a minority of Communist trade unions overturn these policies?

'Labour party members should organize in the trade unions in exactly the same way as the Communist party has been doing. They should not allow their vote to be split by having several non-Communist candidates for the same office when the Communists run only one candidate. They should see that the ordinary trade unionists know who the Communist-supported candidate is.

'The Labour party should also put into handy, simple form the arguments of Communists and fellow-travellers and give the answers to them. The Labour party ought not to allow to go unchallenged in the trade union movement the monstrous attacks which are made on the leadership of the Labour party and of the trade unions themselves.'

I feel these suggestions should be treated with caution. Certainly individual Labour party members in the unions could get together to try and keep the Communists out, but for the Labour party itself to intervene would be to invite the same accusations of outside interference as are now made against the Communist party. The tradition of non-intervention in trade union affairs by the Labour party is, within limits, a sensible one. Conferences and pamphlets of the kind suggested would come better from the T.U.C.

15. *Electoral malpractices occur in some unions.*
16. *Vindictive action is sometimes taken against those who do not take part in strikes.*
17. *The closed shop restricts individual freedom.*

These three criticisms are the only ones which I am convinced should be dealt with, at least in part, by legislation. It was pointed out in the introduction that the trade unions have been placed by the law in a privileged position, but that comparatively little has been done to ensure that their members and other workers are adequately protected against the abuse of their power. Such abuses have grown in recent years and should be dealt with.

Several informal observers have supported the suggestion that the best way to do this is to make the legal privileges of unions dependent upon the inclusion of certain minimum standards in their rules and upon the acceptance of some supervision over the implementation of the rules. This could be done by legislation to confine the legal privileges of unions to those which register with the Chief Registrar of Friendly Societies. Registration would then become for all practical purposes obligatory. But applications for registration would only be accepted from unions whose rules contained certain specific safeguards regarding election procedure, the eligibility of workers for union membership, the grounds for expulsion and other penalties, and the right of appeal to an outside body.

They might well embody a suggestion made by Mr Grunfeld in *Trade Unions and the Individual* (see Preface) that an expelled person should be allowed to remain a full member while he is *bona fide* prosecuting his appeals against an expulsion decision. They would in general provide for disputes between an individual and his union to be submitted to arbitration.

If the rules were put right, a large part of the battle would have been won, but it would still be necessary to ensure that the rules were properly carried out. As things are, members can in some cases have recourse to the courts, but often, particularly where an election malpractice is suspected, a member is in no position to obtain the evidence necessary to support his case.

No doubt it would be possible to strengthen the powers of the courts, which have in recent years been tending to an increasing extent to uphold the rights of individual union members; but many people find law courts inhuman, expensive, desperately slow, and rather frightening. The better course would be to give supervisory authority to the Registrar, to whom the rules have to be submitted and who already has considerable powers over the political activities of unions.

'The man who feels himself helpless in the grip of a union machine', said a leading article in *The Times* in 1957, 'is often reluctant to change it for the grip of the law, but there is already evidence that he tends to turn for help to the Registrar, who is at present powerless to give it. Friendly advice, understanding interpretation, close inquiry, and an occasional quiet warning might well be of more value than the legal process.'

The Registrar would have power to inspect the books and records of the unions in the investigation of an adequately supported complaint and could himself initiate legal action if necessary, or help members to do so. His powers of investigation would need to extend to the books and records relating to funds built up by shop stewards' committees and unofficial bodies, which at present give cause for anxiety because they could be misused with impunity.

None of this, of course, would prevent unionists sending people to Coventry. Nothing can be done that will make blacklegs popular. It is for union leaders and others to encourage a climate of opinion in which the sending of people to Coventry is seen to be childish and cruel. But if a branch or other section of a union takes such action, or imposes any other penalties outside the union rules, that could clearly be a matter for the Registrar.

The suggestions made would protect the individual from unjustly losing his means of earning a living where there is a closed shop, but it would not prevent closed shops. Nor does it seem to me desirable that it should do so. It is sometimes suggested that there is a sort of innate right not to join a trade union, but if trade unions are an essential part of the industrial system, as they are in most advanced countries, then it is no less reasonable to expect a man to pay his union dues than it is to expect him to pay his rates and taxes. He may not like the politics of his union, just as he may not like the politics of his local authority or his Government. But there is really no political issue involved. All political parties – Conservative, Liberal, and Communist, no less than Labour – advise their members to join trade unions. There may be some who have religious quirks of conscience about it, but they are very few and union members usually make allowances for them. Most workers who do not join unions either have not bothered, or prefer to save their money if they can get the advantages of membership without paying.

Unions of course want everybody to join. Their strength depends on it, and they naturally insist that workers become members if they are strong enough to do so. The only real issue is the power which the closed shop gives a union over its members, and against which they would be protected by my proposals.

Legislation should be introduced to restrict the legal privileges of trade unions to those which register with the Chief Registrar of Friendly Societies. A condition of registration would be the inclusion in the rules of specified provisions regarding the conduct of elections, the rights of workers to join the union, the grounds for expulsion, and other disciplinary measures, and the rights of aggrieved members to appeal outside the union. The Registrar would be given the responsibility of ensuring that the rules were observed.

18. *The Bridlington Agreement may prevent workers from belonging to the union of their choice.*

The Bridlington Agreement and its predecessors have been perhaps the outstanding achievement of the T.U.C. in bringing some order into the competing confusion of trade union organization. Strikes arising directly out of trade union competition for membership have become rare. The railway troubles arise partly out of such competition. The dock strike of 1955 and some other disputes on the docks have arisen out of competition between the National Amalgamated Stevedores and Dockers and the Transport and General Workers' Union. But considering the intense competition going on all the time all over the country, the amount of trouble is negligible.

The Conservative lawyers in *A Giant's Strength* (see Preface) showed themselves so impressed that they suggested that a rule incorporating the terms of the Bridlington Agreement should be made a condition of registration. Curiously enough they followed this with a contradictory recommendation that rules about expulsion should limit it to cases of serious misconduct. A basic principle of the Bridlington procedure is that unions which poach members should have to expel them.

Liberals and others have fiercely attacked this. It is outrageous, they say, that a man should be expelled from a union he has chosen, through no fault of his own and indeed without having any voice in the matter. A man has a right to belong to the union of his choice. That apparently, like the right not to belong to a union, is one of the growing number of absolute rights that men are born with.

In practice a man's choice of union is always limited, and the more orderly the union system the smaller the choice. In fact he has a choice only when unions overlap. If we had a nice, neat system of industrial unions he would not have any choice at all. There is only one union a coal-face miner can belong to.

The preservation of order always involves some restriction of liberty, and a compromise has to be found. It would be disastrous for the economy if trade union organizations were to relapse into complete *laissez faire*. In my opinion it is essential to maintain the Bridlington Agreement, though it is neither necessary nor desirable to make its incorporation into the rules a condition of registration.

The essential point is that union members should have the democratic right to influence their organization.

On the other hand, there *is* something objectionable in moving workers about from one union to another, willy nilly. The agreement provides for orderly transfer of membership, but the conditions are such as to make it difficult. It might perhaps be provided that an individual member who claims to be unreasonably prevented from transferring to a union operating where he is working should have a right of appeal to the T.U.C.

Where workers want to join a union which has not before

operated in their place of work, as for instance the northern dockers, the problem is much more difficult.

I think it should be made possible for them to do so, if they are determined, but that they should be discouraged in every possible way. The opportunity to bring specific complaints before the Registrar should reduce the necessity. Perhaps there should be a T.U.C. inquiry first and a waiting period before permission is granted.

The Bridlington Agreement should be amended to allow individuals to appeal against unreasonable refusal of transfer, and to allow a substantial proportion of the workers in any undertaking to transfer from their union to another suitable union even if that union has not previously operated there, subject to a preliminary inquiry followed by a waiting period and ballot.

19. *Unrecognized unions are sometimes prevented from carrying out their functions.*

This is in a sense a variation of the position just discussed. If members find the union to which they belong intolerable, they may wish to join another union or they may wish to set up a new union. That would be a 'breakaway' union, and there is not the slightest chance of the T.U.C. approving it in any circumstances. Nor is there anything to be said for it except in exceptional cases. There are already too many overlapping and competing unions. A breakaway usually takes place in the heat of a dispute, without regard for the long-term interests of the members. It becomes a continual source of friction. Nothing should be done to encourage or help it. Yet if a large number of members are so dissatisfied with their old union that they are determined to form a new one, they cannot be prevented from doing so, and should not indefinitely be denied representative rights.

Breakaway unions should be actively discouraged, but those which nevertheless enroll a fixed proportion of the membership in the class of workers for which they cater should after a certain period be granted recognition by the employers and admitted to the T.U.C.

That does happen now in the end. The Scottish Transport and General Workers' Union and the Chemical Workers' Union are examples. But acceptance of the new union takes too long. Two or three years might perhaps be regarded as a reasonable period in which to show whether the members' desire for a change is likely to prove a lasting one.

20. *The largest unions wield excessive power through the block vote at the Trades Union Congress and the Labour party conference.*

The block vote becomes undemocratic only when a few unions are disproportionately large. If no union had more than 100,000 members, it could reasonably be assumed that the minorities un-represented in the voting would cancel each other out. In fact, since the Transport and General Workers' Union moved to the left, the unrepresented minorities in the big unions often do more or less cancel each other out. But it is possible for the leaders of a few of the largest unions to dominate the movement, as they did in Arthur Deakin's day. Moreover, the very fact that a change in the general secretaryship of the T.G.W.U. has switched 1,300,000 votes at the T.U.C. and 1,000,000 at the party conference from right to left, shows how unrepresentative the vote is. A persuasive chief official may influence some of the union's executive committee and some of the delegates to the union's annual conference to change their minds, but he can hardly sway the attitude of the whole membership. More representative results could be obtained if individual delegates were to vote each according to his own opinions and if on a card vote the union divided its votes in proportion to the division among the delegates.

It can be argued against this that a union decides its policy at its national conference and its delegates are sent to the T.U.C. and the party conference to represent the accepted policy of the union. The reply is that the union conference is itself divided so that its attitude is best represented by a divided vote – divided according to the views of the delegates because they alone can listen to the debates at the congress and conference.

Each organization represented at the Trades Union Congress and the annual conference of the Labour party should divide its vote according to the views of its delegates.

There is, of course, not the slightest chance of this being carried out, because it would weaken the influence of the leaders of the big unions and they would unhesitatingly use their block votes to prevent such a change.

21. *Restrictive labour practices reduce output.*

This is primarily a management problem. By developing joint consultation and a spirit of cooperation on the one hand, and by adequate and efficient supervision and discipline on the other, much can be done to whittle away the restrictive practices that exist and to prevent the creation of new ones. In many industries, and in some undertakings in practically all industries, restrictive practices are no problem.

In Chapter 8 I used the term 'restrictive practice' widely and loosely to cover a variety of practices by unions or workers which have the effect of reducing production. It has sometimes been suggested that allegations of labour restrictive practices should be referred to a court, as are allegations of employer restrictive practices. There would not be much point in doing that with habits of late starting or early finishing, with unnecessarily long tea and meal intervals, with persistent absenteeism, or with the holding of meetings during working hours. They are a responsibility of management, though where such practices have become habitual they cannot easily be eradicated unless the cooperation of the unions and the men themselves can be obtained.

Neither are demarcation rules a suitable subject for the courts – but I have already discussed those. The results of restrictions on apprentices would be much eased if my earlier suggestion about apprenticeship were adopted. Government action is urgently needed over the whole range of apprenticeship and training problems, of which union restriction is only one and not the most important. If such action were taken, it might be found in the end that little problem remained. But of course trade union cooperation would be necessary.

Agreed restrictions on output or earnings seem to be comparatively uncommon. They are very hard to prove and would seem almost impossible to stop except by developing a different attitude of mind in the workers responsible. I will return to that.

There remains the group of practices which is perhaps most directly in the Luddite tradition – opposition to new machines and insistence on excessive manning scales, and opposition to work study, shift working, and payment-by-results schemes. Such things could be taken to a court, but would more suitably be dealt with by the disputes machinery, particularly if the suggested system of independent workshop arbitration could be developed.

This is essentially a human, not a legal problem, however. Perhaps we shall never get rid of restrictive attitudes, out of which all these things grow, until the employers and unions get together in a common effort to increase productivity.

Managements should take the workers' representatives into partnership in the conduct of industry.

22. *Not enough effort is made by the unions to convince members that their interests require maximum productivity.*

A great deal has been done both by joint bodies and by the T.U.C., as has been described in Chapter 7. Yet somehow it does not seem to have got through to the rank and file. I have suggested that this is mainly due to the employers' insistence on preserving the two sides in industry.

But if the unions further developed their educational programmes and their methods of communicating ideas to their members, they could contribute a great deal to making a new spirit possible. Union journals, circulars, speeches, and conference agendas could all be full of the opportunities, dealt with in a practical way, of increasing living standards by increasing output.

The holding of one-day conferences on such subjects, with which the T.U.C. has been experimenting, might be expanded and developed.

Unions should redouble their efforts to convince members that higher productivity will make possible higher living standards.

23. *Unions devote insufficient attention to public relations and internal communications.*

One of the most effective methods of reducing apathy among union members is to keep them in as close touch as possible with the policies and activities of the union. They cannot be expected to be interested in their organization when they know little of what is going on. I have already suggested ways in which I think these things could be improved.

The unions should use all possible methods to improve their relations with the public and with their own members.

That brings me to the end of the criticisms. It may be observed that I have found nothing to indicate that it is necessary to weaken the legal position of the unions, though I say their legal privileges should carry with them specified obligations to their members. In fact there is no evidence that even today unions are nationally excessively powerful compared with the employers. When national strikes have taken place, the unions have not usually achieved more than a draw. It will be recalled that the engineering employers were confident of their ability to fight the unions on two occasions, partly because of the limitations of union funds.

If dues were greatly increased, as I suggest, it would of course strengthen their position further, though I would hope a large proportion of the money would be spent on improving organization.

Where unions have proved dangerously strong is in irresponsible local organization. It should be possible to cure that by more enlightened and determined management and union leadership, but I have suggested that there should be a Government inquiry into the possibility of making collective agreements legally binding, not only on the national organizations but also on their members.

The suggestions I have made fall naturally into three main groups. First there are eight designed to deal directly with the abuses and restrictions on freedom which have tended to bring unions into disfavour – the proposals for registration, an inquiry into making collective agreements binding, amendment of the Bridlington Agreement, recognition of breakaway unions, abolition of the block vote, disclosure of their politics by election candidates, closer limitation of shop stewards' functions, and workshop arbitration.

Second there are a dozen intended to improve trade union organization and practice. A number of these would strengthen the central authority and leadership of the movement by the preparation of a comprehensive report on policy and aims, by adding full-time members to the T.U.C. General Council, by implementing the principle of consultation with federations contained in the 1944 report on trade union unity, by strengthening the regional advisory councils and extending their functions. The remainder in this group are of more general application – doubling union dues, the salaries of officials and facilities for trade union education, employing more expert staff, implementing the whole 1944 report, basing local organization on the work-place, recasting the apprenticeship system, increasing propaganda for higher productivity, and improving relations with the public and internal communications.

The third group would bring some order into the wage system, in a manner that falls short of a national wages policy, as the phrase is generally understood, but would establish a half-way stage towards it. They would give the Industrial Court a pivotal position in wage settlement as initiator of a consistent policy for arbitrators and as the body responsible for conciliation services. The T.U.C. would attempt to coordinate the wages policy of the unions. The Civil Service principle of fair comparison with pay in outside industry would be extended to all public service. Long-term wage agreements would be encouraged.

Lastly there is the suggestion that employers should take the workers representatives into partnership in the conduct of industry, a proposal which is fundamental to the future of labour relations as I see them.

Divided according to the people who would be responsible for their introduction, the twenty-six suggestions are as follows:

The Government should:

Introduce legislation to restrict the legal privileges of trade unions to those which register with the Chief Registrar of Friendly Societies. A condition of registration would be inclusion in the rules of specified provisions regarding conduct of elections, the right of workers to join the union, the grounds for expulsion and other disciplinary measures and the rights of aggrieved members to appeal outside the union. The Registrar would be given the responsibility of ensuring the rules were observed.

Hold an inquiry into the implications of making collective agreements legally binding on the parties to the agreements and their members.

Give the Industrial Court the responsibility of bringing together arbitrators and independent members of wage-fixing bodies to draw up a consistent policy. Arbitrators should give reasons for their decisions.

Transfer the conciliation machinery of the Ministry of Labour to the Industrial Court or some other independent body.

Take steps, in conjunction with the employers and unions, to remodel the apprenticeship system to eliminate its narrow craft basis.

The T.U.C. General Council should:

Prepare a comprehensive report on the policy and aims of the movement.

Discuss regularly tactical plans for the industrial policy of the unions.

Strengthen their regional advisory councils by the provision of full-time staff to provide services to the movement throughout the regions in the fields of research, recruitment, adjustment of inter-union difficulties, and so on.

Amend the Bridlington Agreement to allow individuals to appeal against unreasonable refusal of transfer, and to allow a substantial proportion of the workers in any undertaking to transfer from their union to another suitable union, even if that union has not previously operated there, subject to a preliminary inquiry followed by a waiting period and ballot.

The T.U.C. and employers should:

Actively discourage breakaway unions, but should after a certain
period recognize those which nevertheless enroll a prescribed
proportion of the class of workers for which they cater.

The T.U.C. and Labour party should:

Alter their rules so that each organization represented at their
annual congress and conference shall divide its votes according
to the views of the delegates.

The unions should:

Double union dues.

Double the salaries of union officers.

Double the facilities for trade union education.

Employ a larger number of expert staff.

Add a full-time president and six full-time members to the T.U.C.
General Council.

Press for the Civil Service principle of fair comparison with pay
in outside industry, including final resort to binding arbitration
to be applied to all public employment.

Implement the 1944 report on trade union structure and closer
unity.

Base their local structure so far as possible on the places where
their members work rather than on the places where they live.

Make it a rule that candidates for office disclose their political
affiliations.

Redouble their efforts to convince their members that higher
productivity will make possible higher living standards.

Use all possible methods to improve their relations with the public and with their own members.

Unions and employers should:

Consider the possibility of long-term wage agreements in all industries.

Closely define the functions of shop stewards and shop stewards' committees and act firmly to prevent those functions being exceeded.

Revise the procedures for the settlement of disputes to provide for local disputes to be settled at workshop level, by independent arbitration when necessary.

Employers should:

Take the workers' representatives into partnership in the conduct of industry.

(There are a lot of other things employers should do, but they are not the subject of this book.)

As I look at these carefully drawn-up suggestions, I cannot avoid a feeling of frustration. I am quite satisfied that most, if not all, would benefit the trade union movement. I am equally sure that few, if any, will be adopted.

Some other Penguin Specials and Pelicans are described on the following pages

HANGED BY THE NECK

Arthur Koestler and C. H. Rolph

S197

This Penguin Special is a short violent attack on the degradation of capital punishment. The authors show that capital punishment is not a deterrent and serves no useful purpose whatsoever. They examine the attitude of the retentionists and of the judges. They analyse the actions for which those convicted have been hanged in recent times. Finally they make a moving plea for sanity in the future.

Arthur Koestler's *Reflections on Hanging* is among the most outstanding books ever written on capital punishment. He joins forces here with C. H. Rolph, the well-known *New Statesman* correspondent.

HANGED IN ERROR

Leslie Hale

S196

Has an innocent man ever hanged?
Leslie Hale, M.P. for Oldham (West) and witty protagonist of liberty in every form, gives an unequivocal answer to this hotly debated question. He takes six case histories to build up a mass of evidence which shows beyond doubt that the innocent have been hanged. In the second part he cites cases where a wrong verdict has been recorded at the trial and an innocent man has been saved only by the admission of subsequent evidence.

THE GREAT CRASH 1929

J. K. Galbraith

A540

Since Lionel Robbins's famous work *The Great Depression* no account of the financial insanity of 1929 has been issued in a form at once so readable, so humorous, and so carefully authenticated as this book, in which Professor Galbraith examines the 'gold-rush fantasy' in American psychology and describes its dire consequences. The Florida land boom, the operations of Insull, Kreuger, and Hatry, and the fabulous Shenandoah Corporation all come together in this penetrating study of concerted human greed and folly. From the cold figures of Wall Street the author wrenches a tense drama.

'An intriguing study . . . Professor Galbraith has marshalled and presented the material well . . . What he has done is assuredly worth while' – Roy Harrod in the *Sunday Times*

'Professor Galbraith performed a necessary and useful task in producing a lively and highly readable account of that disaster . . . It abounds in witty remarks' – *Financial Times*

'*The Great Crash*, one of the most engrossing books I have ever read, is also tinged with grim humour' – *Daily Telegraph*

THE RISE OF THE MERITOCRACY

Michael Young

A485

Dr Michael Young has christened the oligarchy of the future
'Meritocracy' – and the word has gone into the language. It
would appear that

$$\text{I.Q.} + \text{EFFORT} = \text{MERIT}$$

will constitute the basic belief of the ruling class of the next
century. Projecting himself into the year 2034, the author of
this telling satire shows how present decisions and practices
may remould our society. Already today it is no longer enough
to be somebody's nephew to obtain a responsible post in the
civil service, in teaching, in science, or in commerce. Experts in
education and selection apply scientific principle to sift out the
leaders of tomorrow. You need intelligence rating, qualification, experience, application, and a certain calibre to achieve
status – in a word, you must show 'merit'. Is this an undivided
blessing?

'Its wit, its style, and its continuous fountain-gush of new ideas
make it compulsively enjoyable reading from cover to cover' –
Time and Tide

'Brilliant essay' – *Guardian*

THE STAGNANT SOCIETY

Michael Shanks

S189

CLASS BARRIERS + TRADITIONAL VALUES = STAGNANT SOCIETY

Year by year, Britain's rate of economic growth has been falling behind that of her competitors abroad. Attempts to provide economic expansion with stable prices have so far conspicuously failed. The reasons, Michael Shanks argues, are not basically economic but are deeply rooted in our social structure and our way of life. What is needed is a drastic reform, not only of our trade unions – though this is a first requirement – but of our whole system of industrial and class relations. It is class divisions which above all inhibit economic efficiency and growth.

After a penetrating analysis of the problems caused by class barriers, Michael Shanks proposes a comprehensive and highly radical programme of economic, social, and political reforms, designed to make Britain a united, dynamic society. Much of what he has to say will be novel and disturbing to trade unionists, industrialists, Conservatives, Socialists, and Liberals alike.

But, challenging though some of his conclusions may be, it is impossible to doubt the urgency of the problems he raises.